John Wayne "Jack" Schlatter, author  stories in the *Chicken Soup for the* with his own collection of inspirat insights and humor gathered over producing over 200 complete theatrical produ... of one of the most amazing families ever known, he will touch your heart, tickle your funny bone and enrich your wisdom.

Three of his stories have had a tremendous impact on American culture. *I Am A Teacher* is one of the most widely read and reprinted tributes in the last 10 years. *The Simple Gesture* has been known to save lives and form new friendships, and it has been rewritten countless times and retold throughout the nation. *The Magic Pebbles* received a great compliment from Jack Canfield, coauthor of the Chicken Soup series. When asked by *Modern Woodman* magazine to choose the single story that meant the most to him, he named *The Magic Pebbles*.

Inspired by Canfield and Mark Victor Hansen, whose dreams "woke him up," Mr. Schlatter has become aware of the countless Gifts left by the Side of the Road of life. In this book, he shares his discoveries with you.

"Jack Schlatter is a charismatic, consummate communicator who will have you laughing through your tears as he squeezes your heart with timeless truths."
— Mark Victor Hansen, Co-Author of *Chicken Soup for the Soul*

"Do not pass up the opportunity to be entertained and inspired by this amazing human being."
— Jack Canfield, Co-Author of *Chicken Soup for the Soul*

"Jack Schlatter's class was like a place from Camelot, some place mystical, where your imagination counted, where it could soar... His writings will help the reader discover their 'kingdom within.'"
— Maura Conlon-McIvor, Author of the best-selling *FBI Girl, How I learned to Crack My Father's Code*

"Those students fortunate enough to have had Jack Schlatter as a teacher have been inspired for life. His lessons, speeches, and writings have led countless students to discover their own inner genius. He is the most effective teacher I have ever known."
— Jim Cross, Ed. D., Finalist *California Teacher of the Year*

Gifts *by the*

Side *of the* Road

HEART WARMING STORIES

Recognizing and expressing
appreciation for the
hidden "gifts"
life's journey brings

JOHN WAYNE SCHLATTER

HEART PRODUCTIONS & PUBLISHING
Newton Junction, NH

DEDICATION

It is with love and appreciation that I dedicate this book to....

Marjie Blevins. The lady who taught me how to learn from my students, she supplied the music for my shows and filled my soul with the melody of her special friendship.

Billy Don Bevill. I believe that friendship is an art, and Bill Bevill is a master painter who uses the canvas of life to create images of loyalty, caring and sincerity.

Marty Crowe. No matter how I "appeared," Marty always saw the "me" I wanted to be. When I thought my days as a teacher were ending, he saw them as just beginning but in a much larger classroom.

And one of the greatest brothers and men of all time, **George H. Schlatter.** His life was one of my first classrooms, where I lived as a student and took post graduate courses in Courage, Creativity, Loyalty, and, above all, Humor. He taught me how to teach long before I knew I was going to be a teacher. More than a brother, he has been a lighthouse who guided my voyage as I set sail, always challenging my inclination to take comfort in safe harbors, he encouraged my journey to make it the adventure of a lifetime.

A painter looked out his window and saw a dejected hobo. Something struck a chord in that painter, and he painted a portrait of the man with one exception... into the eyes he painted a look of confidence, excitement and determination. He then asked the hobo to come in and view his work.

The hobo, thinking he saw something of "himself, the man he had wanted to be" said, "Is that 'me' really me?"

The painter replied, "That's the 'you' I see."

The hobo straightened up and said, "If that's the man you see, that's the man I will be."

ACKNOWLEDGEMENTS

First, I express my gratitude to **Mary and Craig Reynolds**, who planted a new energy in my heart and are my earthly angels... Magnificent! Mary and Craig give like an endless fount of holy water... Along with resurrecting my career as a speaker and writer, they have re-energized old friendships. They have created *I Am A Teacher* and *The Simple Gesture* movies for online viewing through their vision to Make A Difference with their Heart Productions & Publishing company. Because of their work and through their writings, I have received inspiration and wisdom... and more letters of appreciation from readers than I could have imagined.

I truly appreciate the two men whose realization of their dream awakened mine. I have benefited so much from the wisdom of **Jack Canfield**, and in all honesty I must credit **Mark Victor Hansen** for making me aware of the importance of *I AM A TEACHER.* I am one of thousands who have been led to the discovery of my "Gifts by the Side of the Road" by these two giants, who so loudly proclaim the potential of greatness to be found in every human being.

Kif Anderson, founder of Amazing Productions, whose support and assistance inspired me to greater work.

Kathy Abbot Troxel, whose "faith" gave light to my soul.

Maura Conlon-McIvor, **Susie Tellez** and **Laurie Klatscher**, who taught me that Appreciation is the greatest gift I could give to my students.

Steve Bridenball, **Kathy Brick**, **Simone Katz**, **David Brown, Noel Lafin**, **Renee Razer**, **Jim Vance**, **Cora Countryman**, **Jeanne West** and **Jim Hocking,** who taught me that friendships can last long after graduation.

Jean Cross, Apostle of Truth, A tower of Integrity, an Angel to Education, who has made many impossible dreams possible.

Mindy Dow, **Jessica Peale** and **Kristen Solo**, who taught me to allow my students to "teach" me.

Carol and **Roy Bensted**, **Sam** and **Ruby Peters**, my second families.

Bill Pomeroy, **Mark Till**, **Ann Friedly** and **Danelle Bensted**, who taught me that God plays Monopoly and that friendship is his greatest blessing.

Jim Cross, **Ray** and **Georgia Mossholder**, **Dr. James Young**, **Susan Vanzant** and **Bobbie Eisenga**, Beloved Teachers whose lessons last long after one leaves the classroom.

Laurie Crowe, **Mickey Schlatter** and **Jolene Schlatter**, three of the greatest sisters in the world.

Lisa Manley, my personal pathfinder, whose faith encouraged me to follow the path I have followed to create this book.

Ed Gerber, who shared his home and his family with me, which became my sanctuary for creation.

Jeff Gehringer and **Paul Legas**, Apostles and Historians of the philosophy of "God Love Ya Productions" for 20 years.

Sally Blevins, a friend of the soul and an inspiration to the spirit.

Jana Bundy and **Heidi Hamilton**, for being Prophets of Patriotism.

Stan Moger, who for the last seven years has shared great messages of inspiration and humor that have enriched my life.

Matt Diers, **Jodi Frost**, **Mark Vana**, **Stan Scott**, **Amber Campbell**, **Steve Schultz**, **Judy Trujillo**, **Anne Conway**, **Jill Phillps**, **Ralph Opacic** and **Lori Raper** for their innumerable contributions to education, and all the other teachers and staff of the Grand Junction School District who teach from the Heart.

Debbie Schlatter, **Kathy Bevill**, **Gina Schlatter** and her daughter **Syma** for their continued great love and support.

Paul Chatel and **Jimmy Schlatter** for being two of the most courageous and loyal souls I have ever known, and my five fabulous nieces **Pam**, **Kim**, **Jamie**, **Andrea** and **Marla**, who have made me so proud to be their Uncle.

Chuck Page, First "Knight of the Round Table" and Noble Public Servant.

Shirley Smith, for making the past young again.

Just lots of love to my outstanding godson **Ben** and adopted niece **Rachel Blevins Boor** and to their great father **Michael**.

And last, but not least, **Paul Bures**, **Jim Coopersmith**, **Regina Scott**, **Ken Rice**, **Caroline Arnett** and **Joanne Simpson**, for sharing inspiring and wise thoughts.

No duty is more urgent than that of returning *thanks*.

— James Allen

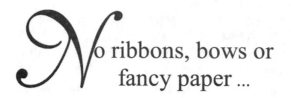 **N**o ribbons, bows or
fancy paper ...

Rekindle a sense of wonder, excitement and joy in your life.

Let history's pathfinders guide you along a more adventurous route.

*Learn how goals, dreams and love can create the
greatest life insurance in the world.*

*Experience '"The Timeless Visit"
—a story of despair, hope and triumph.*

See how to envision your own world in a radiant new light.

Discover how to "dream your painting" and "paint your dream."

Learn the truth about the mirage we call Death.

CONTENTS

INTRODUCTION

In September of 1957, I entered a classroom and walked into my Life. I faced 30 students and saw my future. I thought I had been given a job, but it was years later I discovered that what I had really been given was my Destiny.

Teaching is a Treasure Chest of glorious adventures that offer themselves daily. The more I tried to "give" as a teacher, the more I came to realize that I had received countless gifts my entire life, beginning with those I received from my Five Greatest Teachers whose names are Mom, Dad, Bob, George and Alan. You will be given the opportunity to learn from them, also, as you read their stories in the pages of this book.

During my professional life, I received many paychecks, but far more important, I was given Lifelong Friendships that have blessed my career, Tremendous Tragedies that led to my standing by graves dug far too soon for bodies far too young, and Healing Humor that brightened the good times and helped me through the hard times.

My goal in writing this book is to awaken a nation to how much Appreciation we owe to those who have gone before and those who are here now.

However, it has turned into a Love Letter to all those who have blessed not only my life but Life Itself, and to all others like them whom I have yet to meet.

Over the years I have received so many gifts I had to share them. It is my prayer that, as you read these writings, you will become aware of your gifts, Gifts that you can leave by the Side of the Road for others.

My Dream

I saw a covered wagon traveling along the road and finally arriving at a most welcome watering hole. After filling their canteens with the refreshing liquid, the travelers realized that they had more canteens than they could ever use, and knowing that others were following in their path, they decided to leave the extra ones by the side of the road.

A little later another solitary wagon arrived at the watering hole and they were overjoyed to discover the discarded canteens. After replenishing their supply of water, they decided to leave some of their excess blankets for other pilgrims who were yet to arrive.

Later, a wagon arrived whose inhabitants were truly in need of blankets, and they joyfully accepted the gifts from their unknown benefactors. Getting into the spirit of the thing, they left some harnesses which they no longer needed.

And so it went, each wagon would leave something for those who were to follow and every wagon grateful to those who had come before...

When I awoke, I realized how much like life my dream was... As one poet said, "We have all drunk from wells we did not dig, on roads we did not pave and received blessings we did not create..."

A grateful heart opens itself for more blessings, and an appreciative attitude inspires one to become creative and make contributions...

To truly Live, we must Give... and treasure the gifts we have been given...

It is possible to *give* without loving,
but it is impossible to *love* without giving.

— Richard Braunstein

Of all the complaints teachers hear (and there are many), this one is the most recurring: "Why do we have to learn this stuff?" The next story might just provide an answer.

THE MAGIC PEBBLES

"Why do we have to learn all this dumb stuff?"

Whenever this common question comes up, I answer it by recounting the following legend.

One night, a group of nomads were preparing to retire for the evening when, suddenly, they were surrounded by a great light. They knew they were in the presence of a celestial being, and with eager anticipation they silently awaited a wondrous message of colossal importance that they knew must be especially for them.

Finally, a voice spoke. "Gather as many pebbles as you can. Put them in your saddlebags. Travel a day's journey, and tomorrow night will find you both glad and sad."

After having departed, the nomads shared their disappointment and anger with one another. They had expected the revelation of a great universal truth that would enable them to create wealth, health and purpose for the world. But instead they were given a menial task that made no sense to them at all.

As they grumbled their discontent, however, the memory of their visitor's brilliance caused each one to pick up a few pebbles and deposit them in their saddlebags.

They traveled a hard day's journey, forgetting the pebbles they each carried with them. That night, while making camp, they reached into their saddlebags and discovered every pebble they had gathered had become a diamond. They were glad they had diamonds. They were sad they had not gathered more pebbles.

An experience I had early in my teaching career with a student I shall call Alan illustrated the truth of that legend to me.

When Alan was in the eighth grade, he majored in "trouble" with a minor in "suspensions." He had studied how to be a bully and was getting his Masters in "thievery."

Every day I had my students memorize a quotation from a great thinker. As I called roll, I would begin a quotation. To be counted present, the student would be expected to finish the thought. For example, "Alice Adams, 'There is no failure except'..." I would begin. "...'in no longer trying.' I'm present, Mr. Schlatter."

So it went that by the end of the year, my young charges would have memorized 150 great thoughts.

"If you can see the obstacles, you've taken your eyes off the goal."

"A cynic is someone who knows the price of everything and the value of nothing."

And, of course, Napoleon Hill's: "If you can conceive it and believe it, you can achieve it."

No one ever complained more about this morning ritual than Alan, right up to the time that he was expelled. I lost touch with him after that for five years. Then one day, out of the blue, he called. He was in a special program at one of the neighboring colleges and had just finished a parole program.

He told me that he had been sent to juvenile hall after being expelled, and had been shipped off to the California Youth Authority for his antics. He had become so disgusted with himself during this time that he had taken a razor blade and cut his wrists.

He said, "You know what, Mr. Schlatter, as I lay there with my life running out of my body, I suddenly remembered that dumb quote you made me write 20 times one day. 'There is no failure except in no longer trying.' It suddenly made sense to me. As long as I was alive, I wasn't a failure, but if I allowed myself to die, I would most certainly die a failure. So with my remaining strength, I called for help and started a new life."

At the time he had heard the quotation, it was "the pebble in his saddlebag." When he needed guidance in a moment of crisis, it had become a diamond. And so it is to you that I say, "Gather all the pebbles you can along the road you walk, and you can count on a future filled with diamonds."

Over the years former students have written to me to tell me of the Pebbles they received in my classroom that had become Diamonds in their lives. The following are a few examples.

Think you can, think you can't, either way you're right.— Henry Ford

We teach people how to treat us. — ACIM

If you have no goal, you have no place to go. — Jim Cross

True love creates only positive action. — Mark Till

There is nothing you could want, someone else hasn't got who started off with less than you have. — John Wayne Schlatter

Excuses are keys that open the door to failure.
— John Wayne Schlatter

The more terrible the conflict, the greater the triumph.— Tom Paine

To Blame others for your problems is to B Lame.
— Rev. Lloyd Barrett

The only things you possess are the things you can live without.
— John Wayne Schlatter

If you have a life, you have a comedy routine. — Mindy Dow

In the faces of men and women, I see God. — Walt Whitman

What a person says about you says a lot more about them.
— John Wayne Schlatter

Never play leap frog with a unicorn. —Billy Don Bevill

The fastest runner in the world cannot catch a word spoken in anger.
— Marjorie Blevins

No subject is as important as the student who is studying it.
— Jeanne Cross

What you are speaks so loudly that I can't hear what you say.
— Ralph Waldo Emerson

Failure is not a single, cataclysmic event... Failure is a few errors in judgment, repeated every day. — Jim Rohn

I wrote the following story for the Chicken Soup *for the Soul series. It was drawn from an experience that occurred during my teaching career.*

THE SIMPLE GESTURE

Mark was walking home from school one day when he watched the boy ahead of him trip and drop, in addition to all of the books he was carrying, two sweaters, a baseball bat, a glove and a small recorder. Mark knelt down and helped the boy pick up the scattered articles. Since they were going the same way, Mark helped him carry part of the burden. As they walked, Mark discovered the boy's name was Bill and that he loved video games, baseball and history.

They arrived at Bill's home first, and Mark was invited in for a soda and to watch television. The afternoon passed pleasantly with a few laughs and some shared small talk. Mark then went home. They continued to see each other around school after that. They had lunch together once or twice, and both graduated from Junior High School. They ended up in the same High School where they had brief contacts over the years. Finally, the long awaited senior year came, and three weeks before graduation, Bill asked Mark if they could talk.

Bill reminded him of the day years ago when they had first met. "Did you ever wonder why I was carrying so many things home that day?" asked Bill.

"I just thought you were moving or something," Mark replied.

"Well, I cleaned out my locker because I didn't want to leave a mess for anyone else. You see, I'd been kicked off the team, I was flunking Algebra, my girlfriend had broken up with me. I had stored away some of my mother's sleeping pills, and I was going home to commit suicide. But after we spent some time together talking and laughing, I realized that if I had killed myself, I would have missed that time and so many others that might follow. So you see, Mark, that day you picked up my books, you picked up my life, and you saved it."

Little did I know, at the time, the huge impact that Mark's simple gesture would have on the world. After being read by millions in *Chicken Soup*, it was reprinted by Ann Landers in her column, which tripled the book's audience. Since then, it has appeared all over the Internet in various versions. This started me thinking about how many silent heroes and heroines are going through their days performing simple tasks of kindness that have profound implications. As I looked around me, I became more and more aware of the countless gifts left by the side of the road. One night I had a dream that compelled me to gather all of my observations, experiences and stories together and write this book.

This book is a journey I share with you as we discover and come to appreciate all of the many gifts left by wonderful people we have never met. Sir Isaac Newton said, "If I have seen farther than most men, it is because I have stood on the shoulders of giants." It is my prayer that these stories and observations may lead you gentle readers to the discovery of the giants within you—giants of talent, courage, creativity and compassion—and inspire you to leave your Gifts by the Side of the Road.

To the world, you may be but *one person*,
but to one person, you may be *the world*.

— Heather Darling-Cortes

To enjoy the free online movie portrayal of this, go to:
www.TheSimpleGestureMovie.com

THE TIMELESS VISIT

The man sat at his desk and, with a sigh of despair, pulled the resignation form toward him and started to fill it out. His pen ran out of ink, so he got up and to get a fresh one. Suddenly, he heard giggling behind him. He turned to see the back of a blond haired little girl, whose face he could not see, wearing a light blue dress, running out of his office while tearing the form and laughing.

It was too late to get a fresh form, so the man left his office, stopped for a purchase and drove home. He walked into his shabby apartment, and reaching into the pocket of his wrinkled overcoat, he withdrew the bottle. Despite the pain, despite the doctors' warnings, he believed the contents of this bottle to be his best friend.

He went into his bedroom to deposit his overcoat when once again he heard giggling. He strode into the living room to see the back of a little boy clad in a red tee shirt and brown corduroy pants, running out of the apartment. He held the bottle over head and dropped it on the sidewalk, smashing it into countless pieces.

Totally confused and angered, the man grabbed his car keys and, storming out, started to drive out of town. He knew where the hills were, and he knew where the sharp turn was. Soon it would all be over. No more rejections, no more loneliness, no more broken dreams, no more blind alleys.

When the car reached 70 miles an hour, the motor suddenly died. He reached down to turn the ignition back on, only to discover that the keys were no longer there.

"I'm sorry, sir, I can't let you do this, it would be too great a loss to too many people."

He was shocked to see a young man sitting in the passenger seat. This mysterious guest wore a dark blue suit, which framed a uniquely styled red tie. His sandy brown hair was neatly combed, and his blue eyes seemed to shine with an electric type of challenge. The car slowly rolled to a stop. The unexpected visitor opened the car door and got out, but not before he looked back with a glaring intensity and said, "Please, Sir, rebuild, don't regret; discover, don't despair; reach for the sky, don't die!" He then walked into the mist and disappeared.

Completely exhausted, the man threw his head back and fell into a deep sleep. He awoke just as the sun was making its first appearance of the day. The keys were back in the ignition, so he drove home, where he made an important phone call. A few days later he arose and introduced himself at an Alcoholics Anonymous meeting.

This step was followed by improved health habits, greater quality of performance on the job and eventual creation of his own company. Most important of all, he found love, marriage, children and a family!

Years later, he was sitting at his desk, contemplating the wonderful weekend he was about to enjoy, when there came an unexpected interruption. "Sir, I have never met you before, but I just wanted to thank you for creating this wonderful company, which encourages employees not only to work, but to dream and to make those dreams realities. Thanks to you, I have found the position where I can provide security for my family and express my talents."

The man turned and, looking at his guest, was totally stunned. There, standing before him was a very impressive young gentleman wearing a dark blue suit, a most unique red tie, and sporting neatly combed sandy brown hair and blue eyes that flashed with an electric challenge. The man jumped out of his chair and gave his visitor a most unexpected hug.

"Oh, my new, dear friend, it is true that you have never met me, but I have most certainly met you."

He couldn't get home fast enough, and, upon seeing his four-year-old son running across the lawn to greet him, he was not the least bit surprised to see that the boy was wearing a brand new red tee shirt and brown corduroy pants. He leaped into his father's arms. "Hi ya, Dad!" Together, they walked into the house to be greeted by his blond six-year-old daughter, who just happened to be wearing a brand new light blue dress. "Daddy, where have you been? Mommy's been waiting dinner."

With tears in his eyes, the man knelt and hugged his two treasures. He thanked the God of all time, who he felt to be larger than himself, who had put his Future into his Past to save him for this most glorious Present.

The most important thing that a teacher can teach a student is their own greatness. What makes this a difficult task is that there are so many people in our lives who concentrate on our shortcomings and ignore our virtues. After discussing this problem with my good friend, Marty Crowe, I wrote this fable.

THE BOY, THE DITCH AND THE GARDEN

Little Jimmy owned a ditch. He also owned a garden. Now Jimmy knew Fred and Edna and Agnes and Richard. But he also had a special friend. Fred and Edna and Agnes and Richard always wanted to talk about Jimmy's ditch, make fun of it and ridicule him for having one. Jimmy's special friend noticed only his garden.

Jimmy spent all of his time trying to fill up the ditch to impress Fred and Edna and Agnes and Richard. He spent very little time on his garden because Jimmy knew his special friend loved him anyway. Why try and get something you already have? But the harder he worked, the bigger the ditch became and the uglier it grew.

Now there was one thing Jimmy owned that was beautiful, and he appreciated it. There was a small flower in the corner of his garden. Every day after trying to repair the ditch, Jimmy would take what few resources he had left and work on this little treasure. One day Fred and Edna and Agnes and Richard, in their haste to get to the ditch so they could ridicule Jimmy faster, cut across the garden and stepped on his flower. Suddenly, Jimmy didn't care what they thought anymore and ordered them off of his property. He stood with tears in his eyes as he looked at his broken treasure.

"You can save it, you know. It will live if you love it enough and work with it." The voice belonged to his friend, and Jimmy believed him. So Jimmy knelt and straightened the stem and started to pull the weeds. He watered it regularly and started to take care of that flower. It grew stronger. Then Jimmy started to work more of the garden, plant more seeds and cultivate more. The garden began to flourish. Jimmy also spent more time with his special friend, and he was amazed how interesting and exciting this person was.

One day, Jimmy made a great discovery. He stepped back and realized he couldn't see his ditch. When he looked around, he also realized what had happened. In dedicating himself to the care of the garden, he had filled up the ditch without trying to!

"We're back!" He turned to see Fred and Edna and Agnes and Richard standing there with shovels. "We'll help you get your ditch back," they said.

"Get out of here. You are no longer welcome in this garden." The voice belonged to Jimmy's special friend. It was soft but strong, gentle but commanding. Then Fred and Edna and Agnes and Richard vanished as though they had never been there.

"Who are you?" said Jimmy to his friend. "You're so strong. You're so wise. You're so wonderful. I wish I was more like you."

"You are," said his friend. "In fact, you are me, and I have always been you."

Suddenly, Jimmy realized that the voice of his special friend was coming from himself. *He* had been the wise counselor who had shown the way to save the flower. *He* had been the strong defender who had vanquished the villains forever.

"Wow! What a neat garden. This garden is more beautiful than any old ditch." The voices belonged to Larry, Olivia, Victor and Emily—those nice people, the friendly ones, the ones who had always loved to see Jimmy win, laughed at his jokes and rejoiced at his victories. They had always been there, but Jimmy had never noticed them, having been so anxious to impress Fred and Edna and Agnes and Richard.

So the friends had a party, the flower bloomed, the garden grew, and the very special giant that was Jimmy, that had always been Jimmy, had finally come out to play.

The moral? Go with the love within and you'll win.

Self-actualized people are *independent* of the good *opinion of others.*

— Wayne Dyer

THE DISCOVERY

As I walked one night, I was alone. This I was becoming more used to lately, as I had recently become, a "thinker." Cars raced past me, filled with people I neither knew nor cared to know. I was too busy contemplating the universe.

I passed a small house and saw the tops of four heads through the window. This house caught my attention, for I heard no radio or television, only the voices of four people talking. "Unimportant," I thought, and then I really thought, "What if those voices are carrying on the most senseless of all conversations, gossip? What are they really doing? They are seeking to contact one another. Trying to find answers to what might be considered trivial subjects, perhaps, but at least they are in touch with someone else."

I thought back to how fascinated I had been one day when I observed a tiny ant—less than one half an inch long—carrying a piece of wood. I had watched him until he reached his goal. Was he any less vital to the universe than an architect designing a 70-story skyscraper? They both were "building." Weren't these people who were indulging in small talk as valuable as Socrates and Plato were when they discussed the complexities of universal philosophy? Indeed, they were all making, "contact."

I walked on—humbled and suddenly aware of my loneliness. Humbled, but just maybe a bit wiser.

The *magic* of the street is the mingling
of the errand and the *epiphany*.

— Rebecca Solnit

Being single your entire life does provide the opportunity to observe. I have stayed in close contact with my students through the years, and during my 30 years in the classroom, I witnessed some miraculous love stories and some very sad tragedies.

Love to a human being is like water to a thirsty traveler going across the desert. In both cases, it is easy to be fooled by an illusion.

I have spoken at the weddings of 22 of my former students. I have a hundred adopted nieces and nephews from a lifetime of involvement in so many love stories. To honor these, I offer the following observations...

THE DIFFERENCE BETWEEN LOVE AND THE ILLUSION OF LOVE

When you're In Love, the closer you get to each other, the more capable you feel of standing alone. Love opens the door for humor and lightness of spirit.

The illusion of Love creates a somber atmosphere born from the frustration that your sweetheart is not behaving the way you want him/her to.

Love unlocks the floodgates of truth. You feel free to share everything that is on your mind and in your heart.

The illusion of Love causes you to bury your deepest feelings because you don't trust the Love of your partner to the point that you know you can disagree with each other's thoughts without losing each other's affections.

Love has many channels of affection through conversation, letters, long walks, sharing activities, and having mutual friends and interests.

The illusion of Love is almost entirely dependent upon physical contact.

Love expands your world to include more family, more friends and more endeavors.

The illusion shrinks your world to the point where you have less time for your family, your friends and perhaps even some of your favorite pastimes, because the object of your affection demands you spend more time focusing on just him/her and his/her interests.

Where there is Love, sex follows friendship, caring, sharing, growing, believing and commitment.

The illusion of Love tries to use sex to create everything else.

Love concentrates on the spirit, the soul and the mind while appreciating the body.

The illusion concentrates on the body and occasionally thinks the other things might be nice.

Love is sensational.

The illusion lives in shallow sensation.

Love is complete unto itself.

The illusion of Love requires outside stimulus to feel anything.

Love owns its feelings.

The illusion tries to own the other person.

Love enjoys unity even when physically apart.

The illusion experiences solitude even when together.

Love creates dreams and ambitions for the future that excite and inspire.

The illusion causes a cloud of worry to float over your time together, born out of a fear of losing each other.

Love creates trust, not jealousy. Love is relaxing, not tense.
Love is open, not secretive. Love creates pride, not shame.
Love looks to the future, not to the thrill of the moment.
Love is the result of choice, not need.
Love produces faith in the meaning of life,
    not the fear that life is meaningless.
Love builds up, not tears down.
Love is giving, not taking.
Love discusses rather than argues.

Love seeks *what* is right...

The illusion tries to prove the ego right.

Where there is Love, there is vision and energy.

The illusion of Love creates blindness to opportunity and drains vitality.

Love cares about the other person.
The illusion loves escaping loneliness.

Love creates life.
The illusion causes death.

True love brings you closer to spiritual harmony.
Love is a gift that enhances and enlightens your spirit and makes your life an ever-greater gift for the entire world.

Of course, love has many expressions, and as I am sure you know, not all of them are romantic...

Sometimes, a love just as dynamic as romantic love and even more challenging can appear. It may take us by surprise to discover that when the expression is facing us, it is rooted in the basis of love.

Sometimes when you look back on a situation, you realize it wasn't all you thought it was. A beautiful girl walked into your life. You *fell in love*. Or did you? Maybe it was only a childish infatuation, or maybe just a brief moment of vanity.

— Henry Bromel,
in *Northern Exposure*

Yes, Humility is a definite requirement for an open mind, but we must never mistake a lack of confidence, which "weakens" us, for humility, which "teaches" us.

THE MISS OF A GREAT MISS

I'll never forget the day I saw a *dream walking*. Her name was Susie Summerville (name changed to protect the fantastic). Her smile, which sparkled beneath twinkling eyes, was electric and made people who received it (especially guy-type people) feel very special.

While her physical beauty was astounding, it was her invisible qualities I shall always remember. She really cared about other people and was an extremely talented listener. Her sense of humor could brighten your entire day. Her wisdom certainly belonged to someone far older than she and was like having a subscription to "Inspiration Daily."

Susie was not only admired, but also genuinely respected by members of both sexes. With everything in the world to be conceited about, she was extremely modest and never had a harsh word to say about anyone.

Needless to say, Susie Summerville was every guy's fantasy. Especially mine. I got to walk her to class every day. Once, I even got to eat lunch with her all by myself. I felt on top of the world for the rest of the afternoon.

I thought, "If only I could have a girlfriend like Susie Summerville, I'd never even look at another female." But I felt that someone as outstanding as Susie was probably dating a guy from the universe of Krypton or at least the most popular boy at our school. I was student body president at the time, but I just knew I didn't stand a ghost of a chance; she was too far above me.

So, upon graduation, I gazed at my impossible dream for one final time.

A year later, I met her best friend in a shopping center, and we had lunch together. With a lump in my throat, I asked how Suzie was.

"Well, she got over you," was the reply.

"What are you talking about?" I asked.

"You were really cruel to her the way you led her on. You were always walking her to class and making her think you liked her. Do you remember the time you had lunch with her? Well, that weekend she stayed by the phone the whole time because she was sure you were going to call and ask her out."

I don't think this story needs a moral, but I will supply one nevertheless. I was so afraid of rejection, I never risked letting her know how I felt.

Suppose I had asked her out and she said, "No." What's the worst thing that could have happened? I wouldn't have had a date with her. Well guess what? I DIDN'T HAVE A DATE WITH HER ANYHOW!

So this story can have some value. Please, if ever you are in the presence of the one you feel to be your dream, WAKE UP so you can find out if it is indeed a dream, or whether your dream is actually your reality.

P.S. I'm still a bachelor.

For all sad words of tongue and pen,
the saddest are ... *"It might have been."*

— John Greenleaf Whittier

Loneliness can rear its head at the most unexpected times. It was during such a time that I walked into a restaurant, and discovered how many unseen friends I truly had.

A MEAL SERVED BY MILLIONS

I entered the restaurant alone one evening and approached the abundant buffet with a full appetite but an empty soul. Many of my closest friends had left town on vacation or, in some cases, moved to another state. I felt a lack of support at the school where I was teaching. Another of my romances had just fizzled, and it had only been a few months since my Dad had joined my Mother in eternity. To top things off, it was a cold and drizzly day.

Suddenly, a wondrous series of questions and thoughts uplifted my mood. I began to wonder how many farmers it had taken to grow all the food that spread before me? How many laborers did it take to harvest it? How many different trucks were involved in delivering it to the restaurant? How many mechanics had been involved in putting the delivery trucks together and keeping them running? How about the workers who had paved the roads for those trucks? How many taxpayers had it taken to finance the building of those roads? I knew that I could eat in confidence because of the army of scientists and inspectors who had made sure the food was disease free.

My heart started to warm as I silently thanked the architects who had designed this very attractive and safe building and the electricians who made it possible for power to flow into the lights, chilling refrigerators and heating stoves. As I sat down, I uttered a silent thank you to the carpenters who had designed the comfortable booth and the table that was sturdy and spacious.

Gratitude started to flow out of my heart to the makers of silverware, plates and glasses. I felt indebted to the waitresses, the cooks and to so many more for so much. I was in awe over how many people had developed their skills so they could contribute to the enjoyment of all.

It was one of the most enjoyable meals I have ever experienced. After all, it had been a meal served by millions...

...which brings us to the central theme of this book, Appreciation: "There can be no music without a listener, no art without an observer, and no humanity without an appreciator." — author unknown.

A former student, Laurie Klatscher Lahayne, once told me, "The greatest givers are the best receivers." It took me a number of years to learn that my eyes and my ears, not my mouth, did my best teaching. The greatest gift I could give my students was a sincere appreciation that they were sharing a part of their lives with me. The next few stories are examples of what my students taught me...

A GIANT IN THE CROWD

Since drama is made up of life, teaching drama gives one the opportunity to teach life. However, I didn't think I ever taught as much as I was privileged to learn from my students. Such was the "Giant" named Jimmy, who walked into my class in 1963.

Jimmy was one of the "special education" students who had been mainstreamed, and I felt privileged to have him in my class. Not only was he "special," but he was to "educate" us all.

Drama students are great fun, as they are creative, spontaneous, outspoken and disarmingly honest. However, these very qualities sometimes get in the way of a thing called "consistency." So it was that after two months, the only student that had done every single assignment was Jimmy.

I could only imagine how hard it was for him at times. He was fighting muscular coordination difficulties as well as speech and vision problems, but he never shirked from any responsibility.

I constantly bragged about him being "excuse free." One day, I called on him, and he looked back at me, smiled, and told me he wasn't ready to perform. I detected a slight twinkle in his eye, and I asked him to stay after class for a moment.

"Jimmy, you were ready weren't you?" I asked.

"Yes sir," he replied.

"Why didn't you then perform, Jim? You did the work, you deserve the credit."

He shuffled his feet, looked up and smiled. "Well," he said, "I didn't want the other kids to feel bad. I have more free time than they do to get the homework done, and I didn't want any of them to get discouraged."

As the year progressed, the kids became more aware of their good fortune in having a genius in their midst who was so skilled in the art of humanity.

I have asked the following question to countless groups in seminars: *When you see someone crying, you go up to them and usually say something. What is it you say?*

"What's wrong?" is the answer that is given time and time again.

Jimmy would never have answered with that phrase. In such a situation, he would always say, "Can I help?"

One day I was particularly struck by Jimmy's asking another student if he could help and asked him directly why he didn't ask, "What's wrong?"

"Well, Mr. Schlatter," he said, "I never thought much about it, but I guess I figure it's not my business, 'what's wrong,' but if I can help them fix what's wrong, that is my business."

We ended every year of the drama department with a banquet and speech modeled after the Academy Awards. That year, the students wanted to give Jim some special recognition for all he had meant to them.

I gave him a poem to read titled *Myself* by poet Edgar Albert Guest, which I felt best reflected his unspoken but totally lived philosophy.

We had saved his moment to be near the end of the evening. After he was introduced, he approached the front of the auditorium without his book. He wasn't going to read it; *he had memorized it.* He smiled at everyone gathered, and in a slow deliberate manner he touched our hearts as he read.

MYSELF

I want to be able as days go by to look myself straight in the eye.
I don't want to stand with the setting sun and think of things I
have or haven't done.
I want to go out with my head erect.
I want to deserve all men's respect.
I want to be able to like myself.
I don't want to look at myself and know
That I'm a bluster, a bluff, and an empty show.
I can never hide myself from me.
I see what others may never see.
I know what others may never know.
I can never fool myself, and so
Whatever happens, I want to be
Self-respecting and conscience free.

There was total silence followed by thunderous applause. Two students went to the podium and hugged Jimmy after which they gave him a trophy that was inscribed:

To Jimmy
Thank you for the Honor and Privilege of Knowing you.
Class of 1964

But the story doesn't end there. In the audience was an eighth-grade girl named Cathy Aquino. Over the summer, she wrote a speech about Jimmy entitled *Giant in the Crowd.* She gave it throughout California and Arizona in speech competitions, and she won several awards. More important than the awards was the fact that during the course of the year, three girls told her that her speech had inspired them to go into the field of special education.

In 1992, I was invited to a reunion of that class. The students had made a special effort to make sure Jimmy was there.

One woman who had graduated with that group was telling me of her daughter who had been born with multiple birth defects and the great plans she and her husband had for that girl's life.

"Your voice is filled with such courage and optimism, it inspires me," I said. "What do you expect," she replied looking across the room in Jimmy's direction. "I went to school with a Giant." Jimmy continues to give the gift of his presence to this day.

Every human being you encounter is an

opportunity to experience another facet

of the personality of *God.*

— Miriam "Bobbie" Schlatter

Sometimes a student gives a great gift even after they have left.

THE ETERNAL GIFTS

"Is that true, or did you just put it on the bulletin board because it sounds 'catchy'?"

"Is what true?" I asked without looking up from my desk.

"That sign you made that says, 'If you can conceive it and believe it, you can achieve it!'"

I looked up into the face of Paul, one of my favorite people, but most definitely not one of my best students.

"Well, Paul," I said, "the man who wrote those words, Napoleon Hill, did so after years of research into the lives of great men and women. He discovered that concept, stated in many different ways, was the one thing they all had in common."

"You mean if I get an idea and really believe in it, I can do it?" he asked with an intensity that was unlike him, that captured my total attention.

"From what I've seen and read, Paul, that's not a theory, but a law that has been proven throughout history."

He dug his hands into the hip pockets of his Levis and walked in a slow circle around the room. He then turned and faced me with new energy. "Mr. Schlatter," he said, "I've been a below average student my whole life, and I know it's going to cost me later. What if I 'conceived' of myself as a good student, and really believed it, could even 'I' then achieve it?"

"Yes, Paul, but know this, if you really believe it, you'll act on it. I believe there is a power within you that will do great things to help you, once you make the commitment."

"What do you mean, commitment?" he asked.

I then shared with him the following story:

> *Once there was a preacher who drove out to the farm of a member of his congregation. Admiring the beauty of the place, he remarked, "Clem, you and the Lord have certainly created a thing of beauty here."*
>
> *"Thank you, preacher," said Clem, "but you should'a seen it when the Lord had it all to Himself."*

I then continued, "In essence, Paul, God will give us the fire, but we have to light the match."

A suspenseful silence followed. Then Paul said confidently, "All right, I'll do it. By the end of the semester I'll be a 'B' student."

It was already the fifth week of the term, and in my class, Paul was averaging a "D."

"It's a tall mountain, Paul, but I also believe you can achieve what you have just conceived."

We both laughed, and he left my room to go to lunch.

For the next 12 weeks, Paul gave me one of the most inspiring experiences a teacher can have. He developed a curiosity as he asked intelligent questions. His new sense of discipline could be seen in a neater appearance and a fresh sense of direction in his walk. Very slowly, the averages began to rise. He earned a commendation for improvement, and you could see the self-esteem start to grow. For the first time, other students started to ask for his help. A charm and charismatic friendliness began to develop.

Finally came the victory. On a Friday evening I sat down to grade a major test on the Constitution. I looked at Paul's paper for a long time before I picked up my red pen and started to grade it.

I never had to use that pen. It was a perfect paper. It was his first "A+." Immediately, I averaged his score into the rest of his grades, and there it was, a "B" average. He had climbed his mountain with four weeks to spare! I called three of my colleagues to share the wonderful news.

That Saturday morning, I drove to school for a rehearsal of a play, *Follow the Dream*, that I was directing. I entered the parking lot with a light heart, only to be greeted by Kathy Abbot, one of Paul's best friends and my best actress. Tears were streaming down her face.

As soon as I got out of my car, she ran to me and almost fell against me in a torrent of sobs. Cold tendrils of confusion pulled at my stomach until she was finally able to tell me what had happened.

Paul was at a friend's house, and they were looking at a collection of unloaded guns in the den. Being boys, they started to play cops and robbers. Paul's friend had pointed an unloaded gun at Paul's head and pulled the trigger. Paul fell instantly, a bullet lodged in his brain.

Needless to say, none of us felt like "following the dream" that day.

Monday, a student aide came in with a "check out" notice for Paul. There was a box next to "Book" to see if I had his text, and next to the box marked "Grade" was written "Unnecessary."

"The hell, you say!" I thought to myself as I wrote a big red "B" in the box. I turned my back to the class so they could not see my tears.

Paul had earned that grade, and it was here, but Paul was gone. Those new clothes he had bought with his paper route money were still in his closet, but Paul would never wear them. His friends, his commendation, his football award were still here, and at the funeral it was evident his family and even his body were still here, but Paul was gone. Why? What a waste!

One good thing about total grief is that it humbles a person to such an extent that there is no resistance to the voice of that loving universal power which never leaves us.

"Build thee a more stately mansion, oh my soul." As the words of that old poem spoke to my heart, I realized Paul did not leave everything behind.

The tears started to dry and a smile came to my face as I pictured Paul still conceiving, still believing and still achieving while armed with his newly developed curiosity, discipline, sense of direction, self esteem, charm and friendship. Those are the invisible qualities of the soul here for us to cultivate.

He had left us with a great deal of wealth. Outside the church, I gathered my drama students around me and announced that rehearsals would start the next day.

In remembrance of Paul and all he left us, it was time once again to *Follow the Dream*.

Death leaves a *heartache*

no one can heal,

love leaves a *memory*

no one can steal.

— From a headstone in Ireland

HAVE YOU EVER YEARNED
FOR A PERFECT FRIEND?

Well, who hasn't? All of us have wished for that one sensitive, unselfish, understanding, wise and fulfilled person to brighten the doorway of our lives.

How happy would you be if you had someone in your life who were there to aide you every time you really needed help? Who loved you so much that they paid for your entertainment and food with no thought of being repaid? A person who would celebrate your birthday with more joy than their own? Someone who would take the time to teach you 10 of the most valuable things that you would use all your life? A playmate so clever that they would inspire your mind and exercise your body? Just how rich and fortunate would you be?

Now comes the good news... the great news! You have such a friend(s), and odds are you have always had this person or persons. I speak of your parents. They have done all the things I've listed and much more. For just one week, keep track of or think about everything they have sent your way, from chauffeuring you to various activities to preparing meals to purchasing new clothes to listening to your pain and rejoicing in your victories.

They may have even helped find that one special possession that you misplaced months ago. And let's not forget that most simple and yet necessary of all parental missions...being there...being that lighthouse in your ocean of life. Not necessarily saying or doing anything except for the simple act of just letting you know that there is at least one thing in this topsy-turvy world you can always depend on...

Now comes the big question: When was the last time you gave a blessing to your best friend(s) with a simple, "Thanks Mom... Thanks Dad... I love you..."

Write love letters on living hearts, not on inanimate tombstones.

We not only take our parents for granted, but we seldom recognize the gifts we receive from those we look upon as beings whose sole purpose is to torment us. I speak of brothers and sisters.

My three brothers gave me great gifts of wisdom, courage, humor and inspiration that I have been fortunate enough to carry throughout my life.

*Einstein once said that the last illusion to be overcome would be "time."
The next two stories testify that he just might have been right. The first
one is about my greatest teacher, and the second story is closely related
to it.*

SEE YOU IN THE MORNING

Because of my mother and her wisdom, I have no fear of death.
She was my best friend and my greatest teacher. Every time we
parted company, whether it was to retire for the evening or before
one of us was about to depart on a trip, she would say, "I'll see you
in the morning." It was a promise she always kept.

My grandfather was a minister, and in those days, around the
turn of the century, whenever a member of the congregation passed
on, the body would lie in state in the minister's parlor. To an eight-
year-old girl, this can be a most frightening experience.

One day, my grandfather picked up my mother, carried her to the
parlor and asked her to feel the wall.

"What does that feel like, Bobbie?" he asked.

"Well, it's hard and it's cold," she replied.

Then he carried her over to the casket and said, "Bobbie, I'm
going to ask you to do the most difficult thing I'll ever ask. But if
you do it, you'll never be afraid of death again. I want you to put
your hand on Mr. Smith's face."

Because she loved and trusted him so much, she was able to
fulfill his request. "Well?" asked my grandfather.

"Daddy," she said, "it feels like the wall."

"That's right," he said. "This is his *old* house, and our friend,
Mr. Smith, has moved on. Bobbie, there's no reason to be afraid of
an old house where no one lives anymore."

The lesson took root and grew the rest of her life. She had
absolutely no fear of death. Eight hours before she left us, she made
a most unusual request. As we stood around her bed fighting back
tears, she said, "Don't bring any flowers to my grave because I won't
be there. When I get rid of this body, I'm flying to Europe. Your
father would never take me." The room erupted with laughter and
there were no more tears the rest of the night.

As we kissed her and bade her goodnight, she smiled and said,
"I'll see you in the morning."

However, at 6:15AM the next day, I received the call from the
doctor that she had quietly departed on her flight to Europe.

Two days later, we were in my parent's apartment going through my mother's things when we came across a huge file of her writings. As I opened the packet, one piece of paper fell to the floor.

It was the following poem. I don't know if it was one she had written or if it was someone else's work that she had lovingly saved. All I know is that it was the only piece of paper to fall. It read:

THE LEGACY

When I die, give what is left of me to children.
If you need to cry, cry for your brothers walking beside you.
Put your arms around anyone and give them what you need to give to me.
I want to leave you with something, something better than words or sounds.
Look for me in the people I have known and loved.
And if you cannot live without me, then let me
live on in your eyes, your mind and your acts of kindness.
You can love me most by letting hands touch hands and letting go of children that need to be free.
Love does not die, people do.
So when all that is left of me is love...
Give me away...

My Dad and I smiled at each other as we felt her presence. It was morning once again.

Healthy *children* will not *fear life*
if their *elders* have integrity
enough *not to fear death*.

— Erik H. Erikson

THE REUNION

The first time I met Sam and Robert Peters made me yearn for my youth—their sense of humor and camaraderie reminded me of the relationship the four Schlatter boys had while growing up.

Mothers of Sons are a special breed, always armed with Agape love, humor, understanding, and unabashed, pragmatic honesty. They take wild, undisciplined ponies and turn them into independent stallions.

I will never forget the first time I ever saw the smile and heard the laugh of the woman I was so anxious to meet.

Ruby Peters had been chaperoning a field trip (which was ironic because she was more of a kid than any of her charges). I was waiting at the school for the bus to arrive and as soon as she got off the bus, I introduced myself. Her warmth and energy made me feel as though I were meeting a younger version of my own mother.

If it had not been for the quietly strong presence of Sam Peters Sr., his beloved Ruby, and their three treasured sons, Robert, Sam Jr., and Bernard, Oak Junior High School would not have been integrated, as they were the only Americans of African decent living in Los Alamitos during part of the 1970s.

I could write a book about each one of them, but it is Sam Jr. whose story I wish to tell, especially since you just read "See You in the Morning."

Ruby didn't just raise her own boys. Her house became a second home for countless action-activated adolescents. Ruby and Sam Sr. became sort of like the Den Parents for the drama department, going out with us after rehearsals to pizza parlors or having everyone over to their house to unwind.

Even though I was older than she was, Ruby sort of adopted me as another son, and my mother did the same with Sam Jr. Mothers of sons are like that.

Robert was the majestic "Simon Peter" in our production of *The Robe*, and Bernard was the dignified narrator for *To Kill a Mockingbird*, but it was Sam Jr. who gave us all (including me) a lesson in acting from the soul.

He played "The Stage Manager" (narrator) in Thornton Wilder's *Our Town*. One night, after his last speech, he had moved the audience to such heights that they gave him the highest possible compliment... total silence for close to 30 seconds before bursting into thunderous applause. In over 160 productions, I directed only one other student, Kerrie Stansfield, who had so moved an audience during a performance.

Our Town was followed by *Up the Down Staircase*, for which Sam Jr. was the Production Manager. Everyone loved that show except my mother, who informed me in no uncertain terms that she had come to see Sam Jr. in a play, but he was back stage and couldn't be seen.

All three boys were tremendously popular and outstanding athletes. While excellent students in their classes, they majored in Friendship first.

I never knew what they would do next. Once, Sam Jr. came by my classroom during his spring break, and as he walked in the room, he exclaimed, "My Brother!" My students looked at us, and one of them timidly asked, "You guys are brothers?"

"Yep," said Sam Jr., "but Mom could never get him to stop drinking those bleach cocktails."

When my mother left her body and took the next step on her eternal journey, the Peters family was there with love, shared memories and food. They teamed up with a family named Benstead, and a former student, Marjorie Blevins, to get me through my first Christmas without her.

Robert and Sam Jr. went to Berkeley and Santa Barbara colleges in Northern California, and after graduation, they both embarked on successful careers.

In the fall of 1993, my friend and another brother, Jim Cross, called to tell me the most stunning and sad news that Sam Jr. had fallen asleep at the wheel after working late, and his car had crashed, killing his body.

The entire community of Los Alamitos was in shock. In a world that seemed to be getting so very unhealthy, Sam Jr. and his lifestyle had promised to be part of the cure.

It has been my privilege to speak at the weddings of 22 of my former students, but it has also been my burden and sad honor to speak at eigth funerals. In all that time, I had never heard of a night funeral.

Ruby and Sam Sr. decided to have the funeral at night. As the church filled up, it was quite a sight. Sam had lived as an Eagle and friends of the Peters Family were of like heart. There was a mixture of strength and compassion in every face.

Before closing night of every play that the drama department presented, we had a tradition of the cast joining together for a time we called "Inspiration." Students would share what the play had meant to them and read letters they had written. The afternoon before the ceremony, I had discovered the letter Sam had written to the cast of *Our Town*. I could barely believe my eyes. I was dumbstruck until I heard my mother's gentle words explaining it all to my soul... finding the letter was all the hand of fate.

Speaker after speaker arose to tell what the presence of Sam Jr. had meant in their lives. Finally, John Pillivant, one of Sam Jr.'s many boyhood friends and now a minister, spoke. He said what every one of us had felt at one time or another. Sam Jr.'s death was so sudden that none of us had a chance to say good-bye.

When I arose to talk, I had a package with me. It was a copy of Sam's letter for everyone in the church. It was true, we had not had a chance to say good-bye to Sam, but he had somehow managed to tell us good-bye in his own words written 14 years earlier.

It read...

> *I am not sad this is the last night, and I don't feel it really is a last. I have been blessed with people who care to be friends, true friends, and I want to say—cherish this night. Don't let it out of your memory. If you've seen all the people who have come back, you'll know this is a special fraternity of people.*
>
> *I just wanted to say, I look at my mother and watch things that happen, and now I try to do things as well as I can.*
>
> *Enjoy this! Don't think of it as a sad ending but as a new awakening.*
>
> *I wish I could have written to each one of you individually.*
>
> *Love this night and every night. God will be with you, and my love spreads endlessly to all of you.*

Mom had left a poem.

Her *adopted* son had left a letter.

Ruby's adopted son has written about both of them. Here and now, we are all "trying to do things as well as we can," and it's still the morning. After reading these and other stories, I think you will understand why I was moved to write the following piece. I feel honored and humbled to know that, since appearing in the first volume of *Chicken Soup for the Soul*, it has been reprinted throughout the world in many languages. This is as it should be, as the examples set by the great educators I have known, helped to write it.

Of course, every one of us is a teacher and everyone in our lives can be a teacher, if we will just pay attention. While Mom gave us many words of wisdom, Dad taught us our greatest lessons just by the way he lived, as you will see in our next story.

When you are *sorrowful* look again in your heart,

and you shall see that in truth you are weeping

for that which has been your *delight*.

— Kahlil Gibran

LOVE IS STRONGER

Having a goal based on love is the greatest life insurance in the world.

If anyone had asked my Dad why he got up in the morning, the person asking would have found the answer to be disarmingly simple, "To make my wife happy."

Mom and Dad met when they were nine. Every day before school, they would meet on a park bench with their homework. Mom would correct Dad's English, and he would do the same with her math. Upon graduation, their teachers said that the two of them were the best "student" in school.

They took their time in building their relationship, even though Dad always knew she was the girl for him. Their first kiss occurred when they were 17, and their romance continued to grow into their 80s.

Just how much power their relationship created was brought to light in 1964.

The doctor told Dad he had cancer and estimated that he had six months to one year left, at the most.

"Sorry to disagree with you, Doc," my Father said, "but I'll tell you how long I have. My time remaining will be one day longer than my wife's. I love her too much to leave the planet without her."

And so it was—to the amazement of everyone who didn't really know this love-matched pair—that when Mom passed away at the age of 85, Dad followed her one year later when he was 86. Near the end, he told my brothers and me that those 17 years were the best six months he ever spent.

To the wonderful doctors and nurses at Long Beach Veterans Hospital, he was a walking miracle. They kept a loving watch on him and just couldn't understand how a body so riddled with cancer could continue to function.

My dad's explanation had been simple. He informed them that he had been a medic in World War I. He had seen amputated arms and legs and noticed *none of these limbs could think*. So he decided he would tell his body how to behave. Once, during a family gathering, he stood up, and it was evident that he had felt a stabbing pain.

He looked down at his chest and shouted, "Shut Up! We're having a party here." He had given his body a good tongue-lashing and it worked!

Two days before he left us he said, "Boys, I'll be with your mother very soon, and someday, some place, we'll all be together again. But take your time about joining us, as I've a lot of catching up to do with my girl."

It is said that love is stronger than prison walls, and Dad had proven it was a lot stronger than tiny cancer cells.

My brothers Bob and Al have since joined Mom and Dad in that great reunion, but George and I are still here, armed with Dad's final gift of knowing that... a goal, a love and a dream give you total control over your body and your life.

The *power of love* to change bodies is legendary,

built into folklore, common sense and everyday experience.

Love moves the flesh, it pushes matter around...

Throughout history, "tender loving care"

has uniformly been recognized as

a valuable element in *healing*.

— Larry Dossey

When I remember Dad's victory, I thank God. I thank his love for my Mom, and I thank those saints in white... the Nurses.

To The Nurses Of The World

You are evangelists of encouragement, so much more than you know.

You never let what you couldn't do stop you from doing all you could do.

You are sales-people; your briefcases are filled with a product called hope.

You are explorers, knowing that once you have gone as far as you can, you will see farther.

You are singers spreading the melody of consideration.

You are lawyers making a case for life.

You are authors helping others add more pages to their books of memory.

You are comedians dispensing the medicine of laughter.

You are artists who paint pictures of health on the canvas of imagination.

You are magicians creating real miracles that inspire patients and families.

You are warriors battling against the villains of negativity like King Arthur and Joan of Arc.

Dorothy would have reached Oz much faster in the company of one nurse—for no one can practice your profession unless they already possess a brain brimming with wisdom, boundless courage, and a heart filled with love.

You are living proof that humanity is created in the image and likeness of the universal power, and the name of that power is Love.

Yes, Nurses are so dependable that sometimes we tend to take them for granted. Some of the most wonderful Gifts by the Side of the Road are left by people whose importance we too often ignore.

As I think about all the great memories I have of my mom, dad, and three brothers, and all the great experiences I have shared with my adopted families with names like Benstead, Bevill, Till, Crowe, Blevins, Dow, Abbot, and so many others, I think God is a great Chef.

THE MAJESTIC RECIPE

God has always understood humanity, but the challenge was how to help the human race understand its Loving Creator.

The First Ingredient he injected into each soul was the desire and the ability to give and receive love. And so, to reveal the many facets of this supreme quality and of Himself, He created Families, with each member expressing another aspect of the Infinite Personality.

God is innocent and full of laughter, so He brought forth Babies.

God is constant, unfolding effect and potential, so He came forth with Sons and Daughters.

To express His presence as the most faithful of all friends and his capacity for comradeship, He guided the Sons and Daughters into becoming Brothers and Sisters.

To articulate His manifestation of support, He led the Brothers and Sisters into evolving as Uncles and Aunts.

To reveal His infinite capacity for understanding, nurturing and creativity, He directed the footsteps of wives in the path of becoming Mothers.

God is our provider, protector and leader, and so we could better comprehend these magnificent attributes, He gently showed the way for Husbands to become Fathers.

With a gentle spiritual hug, He daily reminded the Fathers and Mothers that they were to constantly teach through example the power of commitment by never forgetting their original roles as Husbands and Wives.

Finally to this Majestic Recipe, He added the final and most important ingredient—wisdom—that perfect blend of truth and love, and thus came forth with Grandparents.

Everything was so designed that, as each played his or her part, they learned from the whole and thus began humanity's Journey to the spiritual stars, the unifying universe, the compassionate creative God who revealed Himself as the Everlasting Family.

I AM A GRANDPARENT

I remember the day they entered my life. They brought gifts of love, joy, confusion, challenge and humor. I committed myself to guiding them along the paths to success and happiness.

Now they have evolved to maturity and welcomed their own children to the adventure we call life. As for me, my roles have changed to adviser, comforter, baby sitter, referee and playmate.

I offer wisdom as I have been where they are going. I am a caretaker, a keeper of the flame of family traditions. I am a historian sharing memories of ancestors who had paved the way.

I can turn a refrigerator door into an "art gallery" and family chores into "fun filled activities." I offer a lap that is always available, ears that listen carefully with understanding, a voice that encourages, eyes that see accomplishments and humor that lightens tense situations.

Where others just see small bodies, I see gigantic potential that will lead to greatness. Where there are tears I offer hugs. Where there are "homemade" jokes I offer laughter. I love being invited to tea parties with stuffed animals. I stimulate dreams with bed time stories.

My Life Is GRAND...

I am a GRANDPARENT.

The *simplest toy*, one which even
the youngest child can operate,
is called a *Grandparent*.

— Sam Levenson

BROTHERS AND SISTERS

When we were growing up, I never ever suspected how important they were, how vital they were to my life...

More than any other group of people, they helped me learn that life was to be shared...

And that the greatest way to enrich myself was to Give...

They created fun filled curiosity at Christmas and showed reverence at Easter and Passover...

As the years passed they became even more special...

After our parents left us they were the only ones with whom I could share special memories...

With them I could time travel and revisit those times where I learned the lessons of life. They understand my past, live with me in the present and encourage my future...

Thanks to my parents I was given the miracle of birth, and thanks to them I was given treasure, lifelong presents – my brothers and sisters.

It was nice growing up with
someone like you, someone to lean on,
someone to count on, someone to *tell on!*

— Author Unknown

THE FINEST STEEL GETS SENT THROUGH
THE HOTTEST FURNACE

I'll never forget the night in 1946 when disaster and challenge visited our home.

My brother George came home from football practice and collapsed with a temperature of 104 degrees. After an examination, the doctor informed us it was polio. This was before the days of Dr. Salk, and polio was well known in Webster Groves, Missouri, having killed and crippled many children and teenagers.

After the initial crisis passed, the doctor felt duty bound to inform George of the horrible truth. "I hate to tell you this, son," he said, "but the polio has taken such a toll that you'll probably never walk again without a limp, and your left arm will be useless."

George had always envisioned himself as a championship wrestler for his senior year, after just missing it the season before while he was a junior. Barely able to speak, George whispered, "Doctor..."

"Yes," said the doctor leaning over the bed, "what is it, my boy?"

"Go to hell," said George in a voice filled with determination.

You see, Mom and Dad taught us that just like you would never let someone else come into your house with an axe and allow them to break up your furniture, you should never let a damaging thought come into your mind and break up your dreams.

The next day the nurse walked into George's room to find him lying flat on his face on the floor.

"What's going on in here?" asked the shocked nurse.

"I'm walking," George calmly replied.

George refused the use of any braces or even a crutch that was given to him. Sometimes it would take him 20 minutes just to get out of the chair, but he refused any offers of aid.

I remember seeing him lift a tennis ball with as much effort as a healthy man would need to lift a 100-pound barbell.

I also remember seeing him, six months later, step out on the mat as captain of the wrestling team. George's rehabilitation from the devastating effects of polio was written up all over the state of Missouri. No one had ever been known to recover so quickly or so completely from this disease.

The story continues. The next year, after being named to start for Missouri Valley College in one of the first football games to be televised locally, George came down with mononucleosis.

It was my brother Bob who helped reinforce George's already strong philosophy of never giving up.

The family was sitting in George's room at the hospital, watching the game on TV, when Valley's quarterback completed a 12-yard pass to the tight end. Then the announcer said, "And George Schlatter makes the first catch of the game."

Shocked, we all looked at the bed to make sure George was still there. Then we realized what had happened. Bob, who had made the starting line-up, had worn George's number so George could spend the afternoon hearing himself catching six passes and making countless tackles. Later he said, "If I can do that flat on my back with a temperature of 103 degrees, just think what I can do when I'm up!"

As he overcame mono, he did it with the lesson Bob taught him that day...there is always a way!

George was destined to spend the next three falls seasons in the hospital. In 1948, it was after he stepped on a rusty nail. In 1949, it was tonsillitis, just before he was to sing in an audition for Phil Harris, a great orchestra leader and radio comedy icon. And in 1950, it was third-degree burns over 40 percent of his body and collapsed lungs. After an explosion had set George's body on fire, my brother Alan put the flames out by throwing himself on George. Alan had saved his brother's life, but he received serious burns himself.

Following each challenge, George came back stronger and surer of his own ability to overcome any obstacle. He had read that if one looks at the roadblocks, he isn't looking at the goal.

Armed with these gifts, he entered the world of show business and revolutionized television by creating and producing such innovative shows as *Laugh In* and *The American Comedy Awards*. He also won an Emmy for his production of *Sammy Davis Jr.'s 60th Anniversary Celebration Special*.

He had literally been through the furnace and come out of it with a soul as strong as steel, and he used it to strengthen and entertain a nation.

Of course, the four of us didn't always get along, but we were brothers through and through, and yet...

...out of the conflicts came new respect and even memories about which we would later laugh.

THE BATTLE OF THE SOUP BOWL

Loving sports as we did, we all looked forward to January 1, when we could listen to the radio and hear the Sugar Bowl, the Cotton Bowl and the Rose Bowl... but the battle we will never forget was the Soup Bowl.

One February day in 1946, the four of us were getting ready to go into downtown St. Louis to see our Mom at Styx Bare & Fuller Department Store, where she was the head of the record department.

Bob had just fixed lunch and announced, as was his impatient custom in those days, that if we did not appear within one minute, the soup would be poured down the drain. This caused George to barrel into the kitchen and loudly inform Bob that the soup would most certainly not be thrown down the drain, but could remain on the stove until such time that we got to the table.

Looking back, it does seem strange that, since all four of us were by now in the kitchen, one of us did not present a third alternative to Bob's "throw it down the drain" and George's "keep it on the stove." We could have sat down and eaten it!

However, since this ray of intellectual light did not come forth, the intensity of the argument between Bob and George grew, and at that point the fists started to fly. So it was that the soup did not go down the drain, go into our stomachs, or stay on the stove, but ended up all over the floor.

Alan and I were then treated to the sight of watching a former boxing champion in the Pacific Theater of War and one of the top wrestlers in the entire state of Missouri throwing furious punches while they slipped, skipped or danced where the hot soup came in contact with their feet.

Deciding that a better "footing" was needed, they retreated to the living room. There, Bob promptly gave George two quick jabs and a right to the head before finding himself in a painful headlock, which led to a vicious body slam that vibrated the entire house.

It was at this moment Al decided it was his duty to stop this combat and stepped between them to break it up. This caused a temporary alliance as the two combatants joined forces to send Al reeling and rebounding against the wall. Observing Al's fate caused me to decide upon the role of peaceful, conscientious observer.

So it proceeded, fist, full nelson, elbow, headlock, fist, enter Al, exit Al... all to the accompaniment of my tears.

After about 30 minutes, when no one had any energy left to continue, it stopped as quickly as it had started.

We were late to pick up Mom.

Bob and George went downstairs to shower, while Al and I cleaned up the house. About five minutes later, I cautiously made my approach with towels and found them apologizing, hugging and crying.

When we arrived at the store, Mom saw her sons with cut eyes, swollen jaws, bruised knuckles and limping gaits. It seemed that an explanation was in order. We told her how some loud mouth had insulted Bob at the gas station, which led to a fight between Bob, George, Al and four strangers, whom they had beaten to a pulp. (If you're going to lie, it might as well be a whopper.)

Mom looked at them and, stepping between them and taking their arms, she smiled. "I guess you will always be ready to stand up for each other." Little did she know how profound a prophecy she had just uttered. I don't know whether it was the respect developed during the fight, or the understanding of total commitment. But in the years that followed, be it weddings, the birth of children, illnesses, professional problems and even during death, all four of us always stood up for one another.

There's no other love like the love *for* a brother.

And there is no other love like the love *from* a brother.

— Astrid Alauda

By now, it must be evident to you, dear reader, that my mother had a profound influence on all of us for all time. I could use the rest of the pages in this book writing about her, but I have decided to let her speak for herself. The following story that she wrote explains her life's philosophy far better than I could.

THE HAND OF GOD

by Mariam "Bobbie" Schlatter

I was on a bus going to see my only sister, who was very dear to me. She was seriously ill, and her daughter with whom she lived had many family worries. It seemed there was little I could do for them. The day was dark, and occasional showers spattered raindrops on the window. My mood was dreary, and I found it difficult to concentrate on good when the opposite seemed so prevalent.

Leaving the city, the bus inched its way through the heavy afternoon traffic. People rushed across the streets, barely missing being hit by the sea of cars that were moving much too rapidly, I thought, for the flow of traffic. Horns blew, brakes screeched, and the faces that passed so close to the bus were all strained and tense. I did not see a single smile, nor one expression of serenity. As we turned the corner, the spire of a large church came into view. It lifted its golden cross high above the tumult of the street and stood there like a shining sentinel. The Hand of God, I thought... raised as though in silent greeting to anyone who would pause a second and look at it.

Once out of the city, the bus started its steady climb into the mountains. There was sandy space on either side of us, which evidenced the fact that this was desert country. Nothing but sand and sagebrush met our eyes—even the mountains were bare. The black ribbon of road ran ahead of us, smooth as silk as it wound its way around sharp curves and steep inclines. These mountains had once separated the east from the west. Many men and women had met their deaths in finding a path through this desolate region. Now smooth miles lay ahead of us, and we made our way with speed and in comfort. This, too, must be the Hand of God.

The highway led us out of the mountains and onto flat desert; the skyline was fringed with mountains. They lay a short distance away, on either side of the road, some high, some low; some showing faces of relentless rock formations, others looking like soft sand. On some there was dense underbrush. In the gathering twilight they looked like ominous giants waiting to pounce on us. A flash of lightning lit up the sky, and the high peaks were etched more clearly. I turned to look out the back window and saw that the sky had taken on a rosy hue, showing that behind those glowing clouds there lay a brilliant sunset. Limitless, the mountains stood as a symbol of eternity. They had stood there long before our time and would remain long after we were gone. Eternity was within our vision. This, too, must be the Hand of God.

A roar above us presaged that a monster of the sky was overhead. In seconds it was visible as it thundered its way across the Heavens. Up there in that vast expanse of space were human beings like ourselves... seeing, breathing things just as we were. Bright red and green lights twinkled on each end of the plane, and lighted windows gave evidence of the fact that there were creature comforts up there, thousands of feet above us. What kept this huge object aloft with tons of weight speeding through the sky? This, too, must be the Hand of God.

Over to the right a long freight train rumbled into view. It sped through the darkness of night, one heavily loaded car following another. Like some medieval dragon, it lumbered on, the cars numbering more than a hundred. What unseen guide kept it on its tracks, bringing it to a safe destination? The weight of the cars gave off a complaining groan, and a mournful whistle rent the air, perhaps as a warning to some other night-moving giant. This train would speed over bridges and through tunnels, over gorges and rivers, ferreting out its path with only one small human being sitting far behind in a sheltered cab, unable to see or hear what was happening, but trusting to what other men had done. This, too, must be the Hand of God.

Across the aisle, a child cried and was immediately comforted. Again, the Hand of God.

God is at the beginning and end of all things. God is the Heavens and the Earth, God being directly responsible for the miracles that man's mind conceives, God in every moving thing, every single thing, every place... all God—the Power and Presence of God in the air we breathe, the light and darkness in which we live, inescapable and immutable. The only motivating influence of this Power is Faith in Its presence.

At that moment I did not know how my problems and those of the people I loved would be solved. God knew the answers. I would place them all in the Hands of God.

The archer sees the mark
upon the path of the *Infinite*, and
He bends you with His might that
His arrows may go swift and far.

— Khalil Gibran

Sometimes a stranger can enter our life and give us such a great gift, we feel we've always known them.

THE STORY COLLECTOR

"You look like you could use a friend."

The young man didn't even look up as he replied, "Is it that evident?"

"I don't mean to pry, but I thought that maybe you'd like to talk about it." This sentence caused the young man to look and see that his new acquaintance was a plain looking elderly gentleman with a kind smile and a twinkle in his eyes that invited trust.

"Maybe it *would* help to tell someone. Please sit down. Sir, you are looking at one of the greatest, most colossal failures of all time, a three-time loser and more. I've just been fired for the third time in 18 months. Pretty soon, the way things are going, it's going to get out that this is one accountant of no account. And when I arrived home this afternoon, there was a note from my wife. She said she couldn't stand my depressed attitude anymore and had gone up north to be with her sister."

The elderly gentleman leaned forward and asked what reason the company gave for letting him go.

"Oh, they said I'm too talkative in the office and that I upset other people's concentration. But you see, Bill Page's wife had presented him with their first child after two miscarriages, and I had thrown a surprise celebration."

"Well, that doesn't sound like such a crime..."

"Yes, but two days before that, I had returned from lunch an hour and a half late, and the previous week I had engaged the office manager in a two hour argument over the possibility of creating a new staff policy of having secret pals, where each week everyone would receive a surprise present from an unknown giver, so people would have something special to look forward to."

"Why were you late returning from lunch?" the elderly gentleman asked.

"The girl at the candy counter in the lobby of my office told me her son had gotten sick at school, and she couldn't go get him because she didn't have a replacement. So I got a note from her for the school nurse and drove over to the school and took the little fella over to his grandmothers. I just lost track of the time."

"Did your wife give any specific reason why she left you?"

"She said that I was no longer the man she fell in love with. You see, we met in college, and I was student body president and she was in charge of one of the charity drives we organized. She said that when she was with me, she felt like a hostess to the whole world."

"It seems to me that you're more gifted with people than you are with numbers," the old gentleman observed.

"Yeah, whatever. Hey, thanks for listening pal. I hope I didn't depress you. It was kind of you to care." With that, the young man got up and walked away.

Watching him, the old man sighed, "I'm sorry God. Once again I've failed. Since I retired, I asked you to show me a way to serve others, and you have led me to many people who need help, and each time I have been useless."

If only the old listener could have witnessed what happened next.

After walking away from the park bench and around the corner, the young man stopped as he recalled, "It seems to me that you're more gifted with people than you are with numbers."

"THAT'S IT!!" he thought. "I wasn't born to be an accountant. I did it because my dad convinced me it was the only financially secure job in the new world that was so quickly approaching." He had obediently learned his craft, but his joy had always come when he was selling—selling people on new plans for the school, selling dejected friends on their value, selling his wife Kathy on a life of love, learning and fun. No wonder she had left him. She hadn't married an accountant, but that's what she got. She'd married a leader, a salesman and a humanitarian. He lifted his head and quickened his pace as he walked to the nearest phone to call Kathy at her sister's house and tell her they were going to live the life he had promised her.

And on that day in another section of the city, a young girl who had reconsidered her life and decided not to run away, returned home with a new understanding and appreciation of her parents love.

In a small building a shy student got up to introduce himself to a new group of friends and helpers at an AA meeting.

In a theater, a young actress stood waiting to audition once again, knowing she would be cast in this play or she would be on her way to another tryout, but she would not be denied her dream.

All these people had one thing in common. They had met an elderly gentleman with a cane who really wanted to hear their story... who listened with such compassion that he had created an atmosphere where they could think clearly and solve their own problems.

So he continues to walk the city looking for ways to serve his God, showing he cares by collecting stories.

And in the unseen dimension, angels smile and applaud as they observe this ambassador of empathy, this loving listener who will someday in that land called Eternity come to know that while he collected stories, he was adding to God's collection of redeemed souls.

The first duty of love is to *listen*.

— Paul Tillich

Like most professional speakers, I spend a lot of time on airplanes. I never cease to marvel at those flight attendants who seem to cordially and efficiently meet everyone's needs...

TO THE FLIGHT ATTENDANTS

They are your hosts and hostesses as you soar through the heavens.

They are not the flight controllers, but they do control the comfort of your flight.

They are not the navigators, but they do chart all the possible ways for you to enjoy your journey.

They are not the pilots, but they do steer the successful time spent on your voyage.

They work with the Elegance of an Earhardt, the Right Attitude of a Rickenbacher and the Dedication of a Doolittle.

Their multi-talented souls enable them to comfort a child, appreciate the aged, help the handicapped, make the sad smile, tranquilize the truculent, settle down the silly, civilize the cruel, understand the demanding, join with the jester in laughter and all the time protect the population of the airplane.

The carpenter from Galilee, who was sometimes known to be airborne himself, said, "Whosoever would be the master, let them first be the servant."

As they serve, the flight attendants, these servants of the sky, *are masters* at creating a climate of comfort and companionship for you.

And after you have safely soared through the sky, and you depart your aircraft, taking memory of many needs met, you can deposit two coins of great worth into the heart of your flying friend with two simple words, "Thank you."

There may be 50 ways to leave your lover,

but there are only *four ways* out of this airplane...

— Satchel Paige

Then there are those who freely give of their time, asking for no payment except for the knowledge that they have helped to make the world a better place. But I believe there is an invisible payment...

I AM A VOLUNTEER

I am a volunteer. I give from a heart filled with gratitude for life. Even though it is silent, I hear the silent applause of God.

In hospitals, I show people their rooms in such a loving manner. They know there is room in my heart to care.

You can see me in schools, dispensing enthusiasm for education. In libraries, I catalog and process books for citizens looking for bridges to new ideas, dreams and discoveries.

I come from many fields, and after work, I walk onto other fields, courts and gymnasiums, to coach, manage and support the many young athletes, so they may be winners in the game of life.

Despite my charitable nature, all my attention is on celebrating everyone's potential. In retirement homes and villages, you will find me creating activities that help to make great memories and stimulate the development of new goals. Those with challenges are guided to new abilities fueled by my faith in their future.

When you walk into a church, synagogue or mosque, I will be there welcoming and handing out programs. I will be teaching youth groups, raising funds and prayers.

Because my life is so full, my presence helps hospice light the lantern for those about to leave this land for the unseen continent of eternity.

This volunteering is a wonderful and fulfilling gift that I give to myself. The smiles and memorable moments I gather each day are priceless.

My presence multiplies itself in new victories, increased efficiency and unending joy that I help to inspire.

Every morning I awake with the knowledge that I am needed, and at eventide, I drift to sleep knowing that in many different ways I have made a difference and that my life counts.

It is wonderful to give back after having received so much, and it is quite humbling to hear the silent applause of God.

Along with discipline, respect, integrity and love, my dad believed in freedom. A master salesman himself, he turned out a football coach, a television producer, a stockbroker and a drama teacher. He also taught us the value of salesmanship. Maybe someday, someone will make a movie where the salesman is a good guy. Until they do, I offer the following tribute in honor of George H. Schlatter, Sr., who once told me, "Son, I never sold a thing... I just used products to solve problems."

BEARERS OF THE GIFT

Throughout the centuries, humanity has been blessed with Creators of Gifts in the fields of science, literature, philosophy, business, government, religion and technology.

But if it had not been for another group of heroes and heroines, we would have been deprived of these treasures. I speak of the bearers of the gifts, the salespeople.

Socrates created a path of reason through the use of questions, but it remained for his student, Plato, to sell the citizens of Greece on the fact that this was a road that lead to truth.

Creators such as Washington, Jefferson, Adams and Franklin envisioned a form of government that was based on the will of its citizens, but it was up to a salesman named Tom Paine to use his Common Sense to convince those very citizens that it was a dream worth fighting for.

The Scientifically creative people have brightened our roads with new inventions, but if it had not been for sales people, Edison's light bulb would have remained in his lab, Bell's telephone would have gathered dust on a shelf and Ford's automobile would have never left the garage.

From her dark, silent world, Helen Keller served us a banquet of love, beauty and wisdom. However it was Anne Sullivan who sold her the realization that her fingers could communicate those messages of hope and victory.

While England stood alone, suffered, fought and persevered against the mightiest Army and Air Force ever assembled up to that time, she never even considered surrender because a salesman named Winston Churchill convinced the entire nation that that time of hunger, destruction and death was its Finest Hour.

Moses parted the Red Sea, but a salesman named Aaron convinced the people to follow him across to the Promised Land.

Even the carpenter from Nazareth required the services of a salesman named Paul to solidify and send forth His message of love.

Without these bearers of the gift, no factory would be built, no crops would be harvested, no college would open its doors.

Their vision of value, confidence in creativity and courage in the marketplace has built civilization.

You salespeople, you messengers of meaning, you delivers of dreams, you emissaries of excellence who meet rejection, lack of understanding and changing marketplaces, continue to pour your genius into the Lifeblood of the Republic. For this, from the bottom of our hearts, we thank you.

Nothing happens until someone *sells* something.

— Thomas Watson Sr.,
Founder of IBM

Everyone who follows sports has heard such names as Lombardi and Wooden. Coaching legends, they became household names. But there were other coaches like Roy Bensted, Joe Ramunno, Bob Schlatter, Ed Gerber and John Barnes... coaches I have known who turned their players into legends. They are legends of example, determination and courage.

How many victories have been achieved in a science lab, sales meeting, battlefield, classroom, court room and in life itself because of lessons learned on the field, court, pool or gymnasium from someone who was simply called "coach?"

I AM A COACH

I am a coach. I have spent my life educating your children to play in such a manner that, no matter what the score, they leave the game victorious. It is my sincere prayer that my young charges will grow into honorable adults who will:

> **BLOCK** cruelty whenever they find it,
> **TACKLE** every positive opportunity with enthusiasm,
> **STRIKE OUT** against corruption and falsehood
>   when they discover it,
> **PASS** appreciation and respect to every human being,
> **SCORE** with creative ideas that come their way,
> **RUN** to the daylight of building a better world.

And when their season is over, and the equipment has come off for the final time, and the uniform is relegated to storage in the field house, may they never forget that whatever success they enjoyed or honors they earned, they have been part of a team...

A team made up of those holding different religious, political and social beliefs, many races, cultures and backgrounds...

Yet a team that came to agree on common goals which required sacrifice, respect and dedication. And with that experience in their souls, may they strive to make the team of humanity... victorious!

I am a coach. And no matter what their record or league standing, my charges are Champions for Humanity.

During my youth, my most important coach was my brother Bob.

MY FIRST BELIEVER

This statement made me think of my brother Bob, for in so many facets of my life, he was my first believer—the countless hours spent in vacant lots as he told me through his actions that he believed in my ability to perform in hard-nosed competition... the movies, and equipment he made possible for me. When I got discouraged while growing up, there was always the knowledge that the person to whom I looked up the most felt I was worth his time and supplied many lights at the end of many tunnels.

During those years, he gave me the knowledge that someone else still had faith in me when there was no reason to have faith.

So much of what I have accomplished can be traced back to my brother Bob... my first believer. We need to believe in something beyond ourselves. We are needed to believe in others.

The strength of the group is in the strength of the *leader*.

Many mornings when I am worried or depressed, I have to give myself what is almost a pep talk, because I am not going before

that ball club without being able to exude *assurance*.

I MUST BE THE FIRST BELIEVER!

— Vince Lombardi

In To Kill a Mockingbird *Atticus Finch tells his children that to truly understand another human being, you have to get in their shoes and walk around a bit. See life the way they do. As a teacher, I felt that I needed to see life through the eyes of my students. What follows is my attempt to do just that.*

I AM A TEENAGER

Of all the wonders on this planet, I create the most confidence and cause the most confusion.

Mothers divide their time between worrying, comforting, scolding and inspiring me.

Fathers lecture, train and guide me.

Coaches yell at me and then turn around and make me glow with encouragement.

The marketplace caters to my needs, and society criticizes my choices.

While some of us are old enough to vote, all of us are told we are too young to make wise judgments.

I am told that the future of the world will someday be placed in my hands, but there is great hesitancy to entrust me with the family car.

I am asked to memorize some material in textbooks that will be out of date in a few years.

I can be seen planning and working for my future while at the same time involving myself in activities that could ruin that very future.

I make fun of older music and fashion while not realizing that soon beings will arrive on the planet that will take my place and ridicule my music and fashions.

In my spare time, I have been known to create businesses, start clubs and win statewide competitions, without necessarily cleaning my bedroom.

I hurt feelings with thoughtless remarks in the morning and show compassion with an understanding beyond my years in the afternoon.

Sometimes, I mistake possessions for accomplishment, sex for love, conforming to peer pressure for individuality and popularity for success.

But I have also been known to remind my country of its heritage, resurrect a national conscience and see possibilities where others only see problems.

During the day, I can get into an intense argument over sports, music or movies and then say something so filled with wisdom that it stops a disagreement between the adults in my family.

Then there are those moments of tremendous truth when the "ego" is silent, and I look at adults and see where I am going and they look at me and see where they have been.

Then I realize that I would not be here if it wasn't for their courage and sacrifice, and they come to know that their greatest accomplishment has been to give the world "me."

There are times when I am grateful for their wisdom and they learn from my fresh insights.

When I join hands with others and jump into a pool filled with laughter, we swim together in a sea of merriment, totally forgetting the dryness of discord.

I realize we don't love people because they're perfect, because if we did, we would have no one to love.

The continent of undiscovered potential lies before me waiting to be explored.

It is up to me to right modern wrongs and to pour fresh life into great traditions.

The torch will soon be passed to me, and, like my ancestors before, I will carry the fire a little higher up the mountain as we continue our eternal march to the summit of humanity.

Poetry is adolescence fermented,
and thus *preserved*.

— Jose Ortega Y Gasset

There is so much discussion today about rights—our rights to speak our minds, worship where we choose, work where we want, and so many other rights won for us by many gallant souls who were unafraid to sacrifice their present good for the good future of others. However, the focus seems to be on the rights that we obtain from others, and we have neglected to remind our youth that the greatest rights are the ones they can give themselves.

DECLARATION OF RIGHTS FOR TEENAGERS

1. I have the right to do more than is asked of me on the job, in school or on my team, and thus make myself indispensable wherever I work, study or play.
2. I have the right to surround myself with friends who are busy turning dreams into reality.
3. I have the right to turn off my television and sleep no more than is necessary, so I will never be confused for the walking dead.
4. I have the right to live life to the fullest without clouding my mind with alcohol or ruining my future with drugs.
5. I have the right to devote my energy, share my laughter, and spread my love with family and friends and thus create a sanctuary of the heart where I am always welcome, always appreciated, and my highest and best are always seen.
6. I have the right to eat the best foods and to exercise daily, so my mind and heart are transported in the most attractive of carriages.
7. I have the right to see the humor in greatness and the greatness in laughter and to ignore the philosophy that life is too serious for fun.
8. I have the right to be free from the prison of prejudice so I can fully enjoy the blessings of all cultures.
9. I have the right to learn the lessons of the eagle, that being alone doesn't mean being lonely and the greatest way to protect myself from a storm is to fly *through* it and soar into the exhilarating heaven of victory.
10. And *finally* and *most* importantly, I have the right to align myself with that loving power greater than I, thereby establishing my identity on the rock of eternity for all time.

If you were to ask me what the biggest problem is in education today, while not ignoring the damage done by drugs, alcohol, disrespect for the law, weakened families and other evident dangers, I would say that the most infectious disease on campuses is boredom.

All too often students look at teachers (and vice versa) as enemies who must be dealt with, and at subjects as painful barriers that must be overcome.

In the pages of this book you have met some of my fellow teachers who did not have to deal with this problem because it was their sincere belief that education can be the most exciting of all human endeavors.

Since officially leaving teaching and becoming a professional author and speaker, I have spoken at schools throughout the United States. I have met those who inspire, those who discourage and those who bore. From my countless discussions I have come to the conclusion that the following steps can re-invigorate our educational system and inspire students to not only reach for the stars, but to touch them.

THE SEVEN STEPS TO SUCCESSFUL SCHOOLS

Be sure your students understand that:

- You are here to give them tools that will help them create for themselves the lives they want to lead.
- You are not their critic, you are their coach; not their boss, but their partner; not their jailers, but their emancipators.
- The more they know, the more they grow. The more they learn, the more they will earn.
- Free-From is a form of slavery because you seek a negative. Free-Dom, which is positive in nature, develops more liberty. (For example, to be against war usually creates more conflict. To be for peace can truly establish harmony.)
- The lives we live, the privileges we enjoy, the conveniences we use and the opportunities we have were purchased at a very high price by those who preceded us on "Life's Road." Now it is time to leave our Gifts.
- Every classmate is a potential teacher if you will open your mind to listening.
- Most of the adults in their lives have experienced the same fears, hopes and dreams as they do and can therefore give some very good advice.

Teenage marriages in California have an 85% divorce rate. I think it's because we haven't really let them know what they're letting themselves in for after they say, "I do."

I wrote the following as a tribute to married folks who "see it through."

THE SPARKS OF LOVE

They sat across from each other while the fireplace crackled between them. While their "bodies" were still, their "minds" were traveling back in time to that first date.

He was thinking of the hours spent washing the car, while she was remembering how long she had shopped for the perfect dress.

Despite the passage of years, they could both still feel that first touch of lips they had shared at the end of the evening.

They could still recall the growing desires, the building of trust, the joy of touch, the meeting of mutual friends, the sharing of families, the proposal, the plans, the wedding and their first complete night together.

The fire became warmer as they thought of the move from an apartment to their first house, the trimming of Christmas trees, the creating of family and traditions, the joyful announcement of the forthcoming children, the inside humor that only they understood, the long walks that needed no words, the flowers that had been sent for no reason other than to simply say, "I love you," the spiritual prosperity discussed during periods of poverty and the digesting of great ideas after meaningful meals.

Then other recollections entered the room as the fire subsided and darkness became a presence. The memory of the first cruel and hurtful words said during arguments added to the approaching melancholy. Remembrances of how new responsibilities arrived with the children and decreased the time they had to spend alone with each other, of having to deal with interferences from well-meaning relatives and annoying neighbors deepened the despair. The emotional pain became almost physical as they thought back to how perfume had been replaced by cold cream and silk pajamas and night gowns had given way to sweat pants and woolen socks, the week-ends he had neglected to shave and she hadn't removed the curlers from her hair; microwave specials taking the place of candlelight dinners; so-called double dates when the men discussed the pennant races and the women, the latest fashions. There had been her dislike over his pipe tobacco and his ridicule over her choice of movies.

Forgiving his fleeting interest in his secretary and her temporary interest in the insurance salesman had left some invisible scars. And there had been that most painful experience that most families go through, the time when they were no longer the heroes, role models, or teachers in their children's lives, but rather embarrassments, hopelessly out-of-date, incapable of understanding the so-called modern world.

The fire was now almost out, and both could feel the chill of disappointment. He slowly rose and put another log on the dying embers. There was just enough heat to rekindle some flame, and sparks started to dance in accompaniment with the re-emerging light and warmth.

He turned, and their eyes met. Had it all been worth it? Certainly, there had been pain, disappointments, frustrations and hurt feelings, but there had been life—not just existence, but LIFE.

The challenges had created new courage; the tough situations had developed more strength. Their love, which had led to an unspoken language only they understood, had survived all the human frailties and only grown stronger. They had never left each other's side during illnesses. They had helped each other get through the deaths of their children's grandparents. He had completely supported her choice to go back to college in order to fulfill unrealized dreams, and she had thrown a party when he won his company's golf tournament. All the valleys had only been preludes to majestic mountains. Their children had made them grandparents, and in becoming parents themselves had developed a whole new appreciation for Mom and Dad, and they showered them with appreciation.

Without each other, there would have been no memories, only experiences; no goals, only wishes; no truth, only facts; no sharing, only loneliness.

They sat together now, her head on his shoulder, his hand entwined with hers, looking at the fire while the flame of gratitude and love burned in their hearts with intoxicating warmth. Their souls had merged into completeness, and the room glowed while the fire sparks danced.

Some people marry a "vision," and despite countless obstacles, they stay true to it throughout their entire lives.

THE TREASURED DOORSTOP

My brothers and my Dad were skilled craftsmen. We always had a wood shop in our basement when we lived in Missouri. They made birdhouses, cabinets, tools, toys etc. As for me, I couldn't even make a paper airplane that would fly.

In 1949, I found myself in an eighth grade wood shop. Wishing to emulate the accomplishments of my brothers and Dad, I decided to build a bookcase and ordered the necessary wood.

Now, so you can appreciate the full impact of this tale, I find it necessary to describe the financial landscape of America at that time. Gasoline was about 16 cents a gallon, stamps were two cents, movies were 25 cents, popcorn a dime and candy bars a nickel. In 1952, I earned 65 cents an hour as a movie usher, and my girl friend Shirley Reed started out at Newberry's Department Store for 35 cents an hour... and we both were able to save a lot of money while enjoying full social lives. There was less money in those days, but it bought more.

So, back to the shop class... As I started to build my bookcase, wood was broken or cuts miscalculated, so the bookcase became a planned footstool, which was reduced to book ends... and so on... Finally the shop teacher called my Mom and told her that he really liked me and wanted to pass me, but I had to build SOMETHING. Mom suggested a doorstop.

Thus began the great project. After I told the family that I had drawn the "plans?" for the doorstop, they requested a daily account of my progress. Giggling took place when I announced that I had cut it out, and big laughs followed when I triumphantly announced that I had put on the first coat of paint.

Finally the big day arrived. The entire family had been sitting in the kitchen talking when I got home and pulled out the long awaited doorstop. It was five inches long and four inches high and had big hole in it for pulling it out from under doors (which were never stopped by my invention.) The hole wasn't even centered, nor was it round. The paint was smudged with finger prints. My Mom laughed so hard tears streamed down her face, brothers Bob and George had to get up and walk around to avoid stomach cramps while my thrifty Father yelled, "This is what cost me 18 DOLLARS?"

That little object became a family legend.

More often than not, the story was told to great laughter as the doorstop was presented to invited guests.

As we moved from house to house, the birdhouses, tables and toys got left behind... The only object that was always packed along was the treasured doorstop. Mom kept it and shared the story with everyone until she left us in 1980.

While it supplied us with many entertaining moments, it also taught me a great lesson. It is natural for parents to take great pride in the victories of their offspring, but it is the rare family who can turn a defeat into a victory of mirth. Even our Scottish/German Father said it was worth the $18.

In their ability to receive the result of my bumbling with such joy, my family gave me the great gift of knowing that whether I climbed the mountains of accomplishment or fell into the pit of failure I was loved, appreciated and valued... No Christmas present ever topped that.

Every *gift* which is given,
even though it be *small*,
is in reality *great*,
if it is given with *affection*.

— Pindar

When I was in college, I met a young man who proved to me that there is nothing we could want to do that someone else hasn't already done, someone who started off with less than we have.

THE MAN WHO SAW WITH HIS HEART

"Hey, Jack, you're looking good today."

"Thanks, Talley, how are you feeling?"

"With my feet, Jack, with my feet..."

Now, I know that exchange may seem a little bit unusual, but Talley Sanchez was not your usual type of guy. During the Korean War, he had thrown himself on a grenade to save his buddies. His face and hands were blown off and his eyes were ripped from their sockets. However, he managed to work a tape recorder with the two hooks that had replaced his hands, and he had totally memorized the campus, knowing how many taps of his cane it took to get to each destination. (It should be noted that he fooled most of the staff into thinking the locations of the dorms confused him, and despite the shocked shrieks of the coeds who saw this man walking the halls of their dorm at all hours, no one ever thought he was at fault. "I love making those delightful mistakes," he told me once.)

He became the unofficial leader of the numerous veterans who populated our campus, and students of all types often sought his counsel for advice or his company for just pure fun.

"Being blind ain't no big deal," he said. "All it does is keep you from seeing."

Many young ladies developed romantic feelings for him. Once, I saw Talley gently and kindly rebuke the romantic overtures of a star-struck freshman who was trying to carry her romantic fantasies into real life. Tally drew very close to her and his deep resonant voice said, "May I ask you something I've never asked any girl before?"

"Of course, Talley" she replied as her eyes glistened, "anything for you."

"Would you, would you...," he stammered.

"What, Talley? You don't have to be shy around me, just ask," she encouraged.

"Would you reach into my briefcase and get my oil can? My hooks are starting to squeak off key."

After a moment of silence, the two of them burst into laughter. And the now-much-wiser young lady saw life in more realistic terms and became such a close friend that she was almost like his sister.

One day, I came out of the bowling alley across the street from campus, and who did I see waiting for a streetcar, but Talley. "Talley," I asked, "what the heck are you doing out here?"

"I'm catching the street car to Long Beach," he simply replied.

"Talley," I stated nervously, "that involves three transfers and a lot of long waits."

"I know, and now I'm so glad I don't have to go through all that," Talley replied.

"What made you change your mind," I asked

"Well, since you're here and have decided to drive me, I don't have to take the public transportation. And to show you how much I appreciate your kindness, you don't have to buy me lunch, just a snack will do."

We laughed as we walked to my car. No one said "no" to Talley, and it wasn't out of pity, but out of respect...besides, time spent with Talley led either to enlightenment or a lot of fun and laughter.

"Where are we going? To see one of your girl friends?" I asked.

"No," he answered. "To Long Beach Veterans Hospital."

"Are you okay?" I asked, not able to hide my concern.

Talley sighed like one who was trying to exercise patience with an ignorant child. "When have you ever known me not to be better than okay? No, it's the Pity Pots."

"Pity Pots?" I asked

"Yeah, those little cry-babies who are so involved in feeling sorry for themselves about their disabilities that they don't use their abilities. Once a week, I go down and kick some tail...but I try not to cause brain damage."

We parked the car, and since I had some time, I accompanied him to the ward where he served as a volunteer. As we approached, I saw a little boy standing outside, trying not to cry. It was evident this was the first time he had seen someone he loved in pain. As we drew near, Talley stopped.

"Son, come here."

"Yessir," the boy replied.

"Who is in that ward that's causing your sadness?" Talley's voice had a tenderness I had never heard before.

"My brother. He lost both of his legs in Korea."

Talley took a deep breath, "Tell me, does he still have his hands?"

"Yessir," the boy answered.

"Well now, that's why God sent me here today. I need hands and your brother needs legs. I'll help him walk, and he'll help me handle things, and we'll have a party. I'm your newest and best friend, Talley Sanchez. What's your name?"

"Ba...Ba...Brian," came the reply.

"Well, Brian, not only are you a caring brother, but you do a good imitation of a sheep. Want to see me do a gorilla?" And with that, Talley went into his routine that would have made Tarzan's friend Cheetah proud, and the boy burst into laughter. In a few minutes, the brother was laughing as well, along with his parents, as they made plans for a victory party with their new friend. This time, I walked outside so my tears of admiration and pride in my friend would stay private.

On the way back to school, I asked a question that had been gnawing at me all afternoon. "Talley, how did you know that little boy was standing there, and how did you know he was so sad?"

He smiled. "Jack, I don't have eyes in my head, but that doesn't mean I can't see with my heart."

Talley could "see" things that other people only "looked" at.

The *heart* has eyes which the brain knows nothing of.

— Edward R. Murrow

My spiritual brother, Billy Don Bevill, teaches photography at Ramona High School in California. Most schools have only one class in photography, but Bill has five full periods with a waiting list. It is because he teaches students along with his subject. After watching him teach for a day and talking to his students, I wrote the following...

THE EYE OF THE SOUL

You have all "looked" at an anthill, I am sure.

But have you ever SEEN an anthill?

It is so much more than a collection of busy insects. It is "vision" being turned into reality.

It is the "impossible" being made possible through cooperation and determination.

It is a living lesson that teaches there is no limit to what can be accomplished as long as no one cares who gets the credit.

It is Divine Architecture made visible.

When you look at an elderly couple out walking at twilight, do you "see" the romance and the understanding that only years of mutual sharing can develop?

"Seeing" leads to vision, and vision leads to greatness. Before there was a Disneyland, there was the "vision" of a Magic Kingdom.

A family is preceded by a "vision" of mutual growth.

America resulted from centuries filled with visions of freedom.

When a mentor places a camera in your hands, he gives you Aladdin's Lamp, a magic box that will help you create a visible eternity, an enchanted wand that can lead to a deep understanding of people, a greater respect for nature, perhaps even new inventions.

You and this new "eye" can team up with your soul and the gifts of your intellect to help people to really "see" a world that up to now they have only "looked" at.

The builders of the great Pyramids of Egypt only gave us "hints" of history compared to the mighty memories you will create.

At the end of the year, you will have become poets, historians and revealers of truth.

You will have become Photographers!

And you will help make memories eternal.

Photographs are so important because they remind us of all the people we have been while living this life. I have heard that every seven years our body completes a cycle of reformation of our cellular structure so that, at the end of that period, we have a totally new body. Just think about it. Think about all those cells dying while we continue to live. The rivers of our lives constantly bend, and our roads become new highways. Each passing day, brings new life. Let us enjoy the journey...

THE ABSENT DEATH

The little baby looked at his new world and held up his arms to give and receive hugs from anyone wise enough to accept them. Then, one day, the crib was empty, but there had been no death.

The young boy with a soul full of excitement chased the butterfly up the hill to the top of his imaginary castle. Then, one day, the fields saw him no more, but there had been no death.

The teenager cut a dashing figure as he walked the high school campus with a heart full of dreams and a mind brimming with questions. Then came the day that the books of another student filled his locker and his uniform adorned a different body, but there had been no death.

The congregation sat in quiet, joyful reverence, as the bride and groom pledged their lives and their love to each other for all time. Then a short while later, the church was empty, but again, there had been no death.

As he walked into the bank, the businessman received countless friendly greetings from the townspeople who were so grateful for the jobs he had created and the charities he had sponsored. Then came the time when he no longer entered his office or sat at his desk. But there most certainly had been no death.

The elderly gentleman leaned back in his easy chair, while laughing at his grandchild's latest antics, and he knew the "child" was still alive in the crib of his heart.

The enjoyment he received from reading *The Cat in the Hat* to the neighborhood youngsters reminded him that the young boy still played in the fields of his heart.

His interest and curiosity leaped into action as he strove to understand the new computer that had been placed before him. Oh yes, that teenager still roamed the hallways of his mind.

A gentle squeeze of his hand by his wife, reminded him that deep within his very being the young Romeo still sang love's sweet song.

And as he looked out on the town he had helped to build in partnership with his God, he knew that the businessman's influence would continue to have a positive impact on the community he had loved so much.

There had been no death, only new forms of life. And when the day came that his eyes dimmed and his heart beat for the final time, he knew that this most definitely was not his death, but only the beginning of the newest, greatest and Most Wonderful Life of All.

If we take eternity to mean not infinite temporal duration but *timelessness*, then eternal life belongs to those who live in the *present*.

— Ludwig Wittgenstein

While death may be an illusion, birth is a definite reality. When a young lady named Rachel Steele Blevins Boor was born, I was moved to write the following welcome...not just for her, but for all newly arriving children everywhere.

THE INVITATION

The love of two people reached into the womb of spirit and issued an invitation.

An invitation which said...

"Dear Child, you are not just wanted, you are needed.

Please come into our family, our home.

We will give you a yard where you can explore.

We will furnish a room where you may serve tea to *Raggedy Ann, The Velveteen Rabbit, Winnie the Pooh* and discuss the events of the day.

There will be a teeter-totter to show you life has its ups and downs.

There will be a swing so you may fly to the clouds and kiss the stars.

There will be a sandbox where you can practice building your own world.

There will be books that will serve as virtual sailing ships to take you to any land or time you wish to visit.

And there will be music, the only truly spiritual substance we mortals can comprehend—music to bring you joy, teach you harmony, inspire your spirit, comfort your heart, stimulate your mind and enrich your soul."

She can't yet walk, but somehow she manages to step right into your heart.

She can't yet speak, but her very presence says loud and clear, "God is Love."

She can see, and when she does, you know her vision looks beyond mortal scenery.

She can smile, oh, can she smile, and when she does, you are immediately put in the presence of Christmas.

The most important professor I had in college was Dr. James Young. Rather than ask his students to give him answers like they were two-legged mimeograph machines, he gave extra credit for intelligently asked questions. In fact, he once said, "Life is the answer, we seek the question. When searching for the answer, love the question." This led me to create a list of questions I hand out to students in my workshops. I tell them that it may take years to find the answers and they may change those answers many times. But once they do, they will have a strong sense of direction for the rest of their journey.

A List Of Questions To Guide You In Your Quest For Life

What do you love doing so much that you would do it for your life's work if you didn't have to get paid?

What would you attempt to do if you knew you could not fail?

What is your reason for living and what would be your price for dying?

If you could travel back in time and change one thing in history, what would it be?

What are your personal definitions for the following words: love, friend, success, life, marriage, family, education, hero and God?

Who do you think are the five greatest people who ever lived and why?

What movie, song, book, thought and event have had the biggest influence on your life?

What is your philosophy of life? Write it out in five sentences.

What are the blessings that you have received? Make a "gratitude list."

What qualities are you developing to attract love into your life?

What do you want people to say about you at your funeral?

Finally, if you could get the whole world to believe one thing, what would it be?

I was once given the privilege of speaking at an awards dinner for Soroptimists. Story after story of courageous women overcoming tremendous odds and of the help they received from this wonderful organization touched my soul. I was one of three men in a room filled with women who were driven by something that can only be described as Divine. I was moved to write the following.

WHAT IS A SOROPTIMIST?

Someone who plants seeds in what appears to be barren ground and transforms that ground into a blossoming garden of Love, Faith, and Accomplishment.

Someone who spells impossible, I'm Possible. Where others see problems, a Soroptimist sees possibilities.

Someone who dreams paintings then paints dreams.

Someone who is a runner, a coach and a winner in the most important race of all...the Human Race.

Someone whose vision of victory can raise up the vanquished to new effort.

Someone who is so filled with Hope, they inspire everyone to be heroically helpful.

Someone who doesn't just "change" circumstances, but, with courage, "creates" circumstances that turn possible failure into a fantastic flight to a fabulous future.

Someone whose greatness is experienced in gentleness.

Soroptimists are truly *someone*.

Someone who is living proof that there is a Divine spark in all of us that can set off rockets of right action that can heal the world.

Positive things *happen* to positive *people*.

— Sarah Beeny

By now, you can tell that I have been very fortunate to know some true heroes and heroines in my life. They are of various cultures, politics, religions and interests. But they all have one thing in common: They have overcome mountains.

THE MOUNTAIN BECOMERS

Have you ever noticed that when God plants a mountain, He puts it between two valleys?

It is ironic that the higher the mountain, the deeper the valleys.

You, the courageous climbers, have walked through the lowlands with a strength and grace similar to that of eagles as they soar through the sky.

You have used your tears as spiritual ink to write love letters to us all.

You have turned your pain into symphonies of Friendship.

You have used your confusion to carve a path of truth through a landscape of turmoil.

Your disappointments have molded hearts of compassion and understanding for everyone who has had the good fortune to know you.

Your doubts and questions have gone through the furnace of deeply felt prayer to build a Cathedral of Faith.

Most people dream of scaling a mountain during their lifetime,

But, dear, special, precious Friends,

You have *Become* Mountains!

We *acquire* the strength we have *overcome*.

— Ralph Waldo Emerson

As we climb those mountains there is one truth that we must learn— one truth that runs counter to popular opinion... That truth is this... LIFE IS NOT FAIR. But the good news is... LIFE IS JUST.

THE PAYOFF

"Help, I'm in desperate need!"

Those were the first words the young man heard as he sat in his beautiful house behind his magnificent desk. After hearing all of the details of his friend's plight, he immediately wrote out a generous check and drove to the post office in his brand new car and mailed it by express.

Weeks followed, and there was no reply from his friend, not even a thank you note.

"I'm so glad to see you," said the minister to the young man. "You have been so generous in your tithes, but right now I need your leadership for a fund raiser to finish our new recreation hall." Our hero poured himself into the task, not only raising money, but also volunteering his talents in the various work parties that were required. He knew how important this project would be for the countless youths who needed a healthy, safe place to exercise and socialize.

The project was finished in record time. However, when the church bulletin came out, there was a glowing tribute to the minister and the major financial contributors. Due to "an editorial oversight," there was no mention of our young man.

That Sunday could have been very depressing except for the fact that his loving wife and three delightful children threw a surprise birthday party for him.

The following week, he was leaving his place of business after another fantastically successful day when one of his colleagues asked the young man if he could drive him to a town 100 miles away to pick up a new car. Despite the weariness he felt, he canceled his plans for a quiet dinner with his wife and granted the favor.

One month later, he learned that some jealous people had created vicious gossip about him in an attempt to slow down his rapid climb up the ladder of success. What was really disturbing was the fact that the main culprit had been the recipient of the 200-mile kindness.

After telling his wife of his recent promotion, he also complained about the recent negative incidents.

"I just don't understand the rules," he said. "It seems no matter what I do, I end up with no gratitude, no recognition and not even any loyalty."

Oh, thou generous but foolish man. How can a heart so full of love keep company with a mind that misses such an obvious truth?

To Give, to Help, to Care...these tasks are the work of God, and the reward seldom comes from the direction you send these gifts. But as you comfortably drive home and walk your healthy body into your beautiful house to be greeted by your devoted wife and wonderful family with news about the positive excitement you have experienced in the job you enjoy so much, ask yourself: Did all of this good in your life just happen by accident? Or could it have been created by loving actions given by your True Employer, Spiritual Guide and Partner?

No act of *kindness*,

no matter how small,

is ever wasted.

— Aesop ~600BC

85

I AM A FIREFIGHTER

I dare to face danger daily...

I can walk into raging, life-threatening fires, because within my heart there beats a flame for humanity...

When I rescue a child, I am saving some parent's contribution to eternity...

When I carry a mother from danger, I carry the Heart of a Home...

When I save the life of a father, I am keeping the ship of a family safe so it so it can sail the difficult seas of challenge and adventure...

Ceilings may fall, but my resolve stands high...

Walls may collapse, but not before I have completed my mission...

I battle disaster and prevent death from entering lives too early...

I belong to a band of brothers and sisters who are unified in our faith that every life has meaning and therefore must be saved no matter what the risk...

While I put out flames I struggle to keep the Light alive...

It is my prayer that the lives I save will go on to serve the world, thus validating the struggles and sacrifices made by my comrades and me...

I fight fires to keep the warmth of humanity alive... and to promote the love of the human family...

When our *perils* are past,
shall our *gratitude* sleep?

— George Canning

An ode to those priceless Postal Workers...

HOW DO THEY DO IT?

I mailed a letter today.

I perform a huge act of trust in mailing a letter that contains an important message to a very important person in my life. The success of many future projects depends on that letter reaching its destination.

I walked out of the post office without an ounce of worry.

Why? Because the post office has never failed me yet! In my life, I have probably sent and received thousands of pieces of mail. Every one of them had experienced a successful journey. I am one of hundreds of millions of people who have had the same experience.

How do they do it?

There are 50 states, each divided into counties. Every county is divided into cities. Every city has roads, avenues, streets, boulevards and post offices boxes. I knew that my letter would "get there." After all, I had entrusted my letter to a time-honored friend who has never let me down.

The salary of a postal work is set. There are no raises for performance beyond the call of duty. Yet, it seems they all do it.

Where do they find these selfless servants who sort, literally, tons of letters and packages so they will reach the right destination?

Each carrier approaches house after house, business after business, apartment after apartment. Whether there are upset animals, angry gangs or rash drivers, they complete their mission. It may be so hot that the heat comes right through their shoes or so cold the breath almost freezes as it exits the mouth.

STILL THEY DELIVER.

Where do they get such people? For centuries, postal workers have been the veins and arteries of American businesses, families and governments.

Yes, today as I mailed a letter, I put part of my future in the hands of a postal worker. A true public servant, who is Dedicated to Detail and who Carries Courage in a mail bag.

I really consider myself fortunate because, during my college days, I was privileged to know a living, walking, talking legend that inspired everyone he met. As student body president, I could spend time with this gentle genius of humanity—which brings me to one of the greatest gifts I ever received, one that so enriched my attitude that it was responsible for my having a successful teaching career.

WINNER OF THE RACE

California is blessed with many remarkable colleges, but none of them are more beautiful than George Pepperdine University near Malibu. Along with the stunning scenic beauty, there are some of the most modern and beautiful buildings to be found anywhere in the United States.

However, this was not always the case. There was a time when this magnificent college had three buildings, one auditorium, two dorms, some science labs, a gymnasium and an athletic field. Founded in the late 1930s by a Christian businessman, the college that bore his name could be found just off 79th Street in Los Angeles and boasted of a student body numbering around nine hundred to a thousand students.

Those of us who attended the college during the '40s and '50s look back on that time as the "Golden Age" of Pepperdine. While under the administration of the Church of Christ, the school welcomed people of all faiths, free and open discussion was widely encouraged, and respect was shown to all. By the time one became a senior, every professor knew you by name and their office doors were always open for consultation and guidance. Those who attended night classes could hear various fraternities and sororities singing while practicing for the upcoming choral competition. The school was filled with many beloved traditions that were cherished by all the students.

Many people were responsible for this marvel in miniature, but probably most of the credit could go to one of the most gentle and wise souls to ever walk the planet, our Dean, Dr. E. V. Pullias.

Dr. Pullias started as a psychology professor and become one of the forerunners in the field of Mental Hygiene. He was easily the most famous member of the staff. And by the end of your freshman year, he knew your name and your major and your dreams. Time spent in his presence was a treasure every student sought.

Robert Frost would have loved him, as he continually took *The Road Less Traveled*. Looking like a young version of Albert Einstein, he could be seen riding up to his office on his 10-year-old bicycle in his chosen "suit for the week." He had a gentle southern style of talking which made it easy to follow his train of thought as he dealt with some of the most complex questions of psychology, world events and campus life.

Now, there were many reasons for wanting to be student body president of this school, but one of the chief advantages was that you were guaranteed time with this sage on a one-to-one basis.

After my election, I arrived at Dr. Pullias' office for our appointment a full 30 minutes early. He warmly welcomed me into his "sanctuary," as he called it. That first day, he was to give me an observation and advice that would last me a lifetime.

"Jack," he said, "I was pleased to see you win, and as the last of four Schlatters to attend this institution, I know you'll do us proud. Now, I've noticed you are a fighter for what you believe in; in fact, I believe you come from a family of fighters, even your most charming Mother. But, Jack, remember this. A man is only good for so many conflicts, and each one you engage in weakens you for the ones to follow. So I say to you with all my heart, Son, CHOOSE YOUR BATTLES WISELY."

I didn't have the sense or self-discipline to always follow his advice, but the times I did, it paid rich dividends in successful victories. We rewrote the student government constitution. We beat the University of Southern California, U.C.L.A. and every other college in Southern California in the competition to see who created the most inspirational celebration of our Bill Of Rights. We raised money for charity and had many very happy and successful social events throughout the year. One reason for our success was that, armed with Dr. Pullias' "wisdom," we never attacked lizards while dinosaurs roamed the land of challenge.

Over the years, the population around the campus changed its ethnic population, as "white flight" became the standard for most homeowner's behavior. But there was one house that never changed hands. You guessed it—Dr. Pullias saw no reason to move as long as he had "people" for neighbors. And just as had been the case in the '40s and '50s, he remained the most beloved human being in the entire community.

You see, Dr. Pullias was not an athlete, but he was a *winner* and never failed to be the champion of the biggest and most important race of all... THE HUMAN RACE.

... Two roads diverged in a wood, and I,

I took the one less traveled by,

And that has made *all the difference*.

— Robert Frost

CHILDREN, ADULTS AND MONOPOLY

If one teaches long enough, one becomes a time traveler. Watching countless 12-year-olds trade in their young bodies for newer models called teenager, adult, husband, wife, parent, and now in some cases grandparent, causes the past, present and future to blend into one moment. This is both a painful and pleasurable experience. It makes you wonder why it was not arranged so that youth could know and age could live. In Monopoly, once you take a turn around the board, you get to throw the dice again and take another trip and maybe rectify the mistakes you made the first time. But in life, once you get to those blue squares of wisdom, you realize "excuses are the keys that open the door to failure," "the only way to have a friend is to be one" and "there is no failure except for no longer trying." Once you get to those "blue squares of wisdom" in real life, your "Go" has turned into a "Stop," because you don't get to go around again.

So, to all of you who are about to start your journey, I say: dress up your Barbies, but pay more attention to people than to dolls. Send your G.I. Joes into battle, but arm yourself with wisdom, not toy soldiers. Visit Oz, but don't be fooled by fantasy, rather, develop your imagination. Wait for Santa, but remember that there is more joy in giving than receiving. Sing your songs of life loudly and strongly. Sing from your heart and spirit, not just your mind and mouth.

As I sit in this body that seems to be aging, I suddenly remember the words of a great teacher. "The body is only a temporary space suit for the soul." Deep inside this soul I feel the stirring of a child who has lain sleeping for many years. "You know I'm not dead," the child whispers. "I've just been hanging around waiting for you to rediscover me. With your new wisdom and my energy, I'll bet you, if we played again, we could win." And slowly that "Stop" turns into a "Go," and I pick up the dice of life and throw them for one more turn.

Sometimes, the little conversations held in families can produce profound effects and remembrances that last a lifetime.

LEGACY OF LOVE

Alan, my brother, was dying, and I was stuck in traffic. Four years prior he had been healed of cancer, but now it was back and attacking with a tremendous ferocity.

We had accepted the fact that we might lose him, and he was so accepting of where he must go. It wasn't worrying about his feeling secure about dying that was causing me to race to the hospital.

The Schlatter guys had been close since all four of us had arrived on this planet, but this closeness was guarded by a silent code. There was nothing we would not do for each other—except be serious.

We were "manly men," and no sentiment was to pass between us. We did have individual tender moments with Mom, but that only after we were sure that the other three weren't within sight or earshot.

But Alan and I had had one special moment years ago. He had just returned from his stint in the navy, and as older brothers are prone to do, he was attempting to give me some advice.

"Why don't you just shut up," I said. "I don't care what you think."

"That's a shame, Jack, because I care what you think, what you believe, what you dream and what you do. We're brothers, and at night when I stood the late watch with nothing but sea and sky to keep me company, I came to realize how special you guys are to me. We share memories that no one else will fully understand because we know. We know each other. Out there on that deck, I realized how lucky I was to have three life-long companions who grew up with me and were there the day of my first football game and the day of my first wrestling match. Who made me laugh the day Joanne broke up with me. Who told me every joke I've ever known. Who will be there the day I get married and the days my children will be born, and even on the day I die if I go first."

"Fat chance of that happening," I joked. "You're the toughest of the four."

I never forgot what he said, but it didn't really sink in until I started teaching. Brothers are more than friends. Brothers are special. One of the things I know I did do right was to help each group of young men I coached, taught or directed become a band of brothers.

Those two minutes had affected my whole life, and I had never told him. Now he was about to leave us, and if I didn't get there in time, he'd never know.

When I arrived at the hospital, Alan was sleeping as peacefully as could be expected for someone in the last stages of cancer.

When he awoke, I told him how he had made me truly appreciate family and how his talk had inspired me in my teaching career.

"I know, Jackie. I could see it. You don't have to tell me."

"Oh yes I do," I said through the tears. "You need to know that your spirit will be in every classroom, on every stage and in every lecture hall I enter. Thank you, thank you so much, my brother."

A little later, Bob and George arrived, and we resumed our normal "non-serious" jargon.

It wasn't long after that day that he left us, and as he predicted, all four of us were there together the day he died. No, correct that, the day his body died. Alan's spirit is alive and well whenever I speak, teach or direct.

I'm so glad I had the opportunity to tell him. When we were growing up, I believed he would outlive all of us. He weighed 154 pounds and wrestled heavyweight, losing only two matches in four years. He took the state championship in the 175 pound weight division. As the kids would say, "He was one strong dude." But you just never know.

Do all of the important people in your life know how much you treasure them? Don't take it for granted that they know.

In memory of Alan I guess all I can say is...

Write feelings of appreciation on hearts, not tombstones.

There is an immeasurable distance
between late and *too late*.

— Og Mandino

Like most Americans born in this century, I devoted a lot of my time and energy in trying to be noticed. Life had kindly placed me in a family of All-Stars.

THE MOST IMPORTANT EVENING IN MY LIFE

My Mother was a virtuoso on the violin and had traveled throughout the United States, performing on the same stage as William Jennings Bryan, the only man to be nominated by a major political party for the presidency three times. She would give a short concert before he would speak.

My Dad was a master salesman who sat in on meetings with Thomas Edison and Henry Ford. He was a personal friend of Vash Young and Vernon Bigelow, two men who wrote some of the first self-help books in America. On top of his tremendous success in business, my Dad had memorized the world and could talk about almost any subject with great authority.

My brother Bob, a quick wit who earned letters in football, basketball, and baseball, was a gifted trombonist and artist. As a teacher, football coach and high school counselor, he won about every award a teacher could win for his outstanding contributions to education.

Brother George, a high school wrestling champion and all-league tackle in football, possessed a voice so powerful that he was one of the youngest singers to perform with the St. Louis Municipal Opera. After his courageous victories recounted in "The Finest Steel Gets Sent Through the Hottest Furnace," he went on to be one of the most important and innovative television producers in history, creating such shows as *Laugh In*, *Real People* and the *American Comedy Awards* (not to mention having a successful 55-year marriage, an astounding accomplishment in the fast paced world of Hollywood).

Brother Al, who had saved George's life, was also a State Wrestling Champion and had seven varsity letters to his credit in football and wrestling. He was a fantastic magician and had a beautiful singing voice. Before he passed away, he had become a tremendously successful stockbroker.

Then there was *Me*. Born much later, when Mom and Dad were 40, and not anywhere near as talented in sports or music as my brothers, I wasted a lot of time trying to be "them." This is not to say that I was not happy. I used what they had taught me to have success in drama, student government and to some degree in sports. Being born into that family was a wonderful gift from life, but because I kept comparing myself with them, my self-confidence was below "see level."

However, one night my whole life changed in 45 minutes.

I had come home early from a party where hardly anyone had noticed I was there, except for a couple of times when I made a fool of myself trying to get attention.

Like George Gobel once said about himself on *The Tonight Show*, "I felt like the whole world was a tuxedo and I was a pair of brown shoes." (Or I felt like a duck trying to get the attention of swans.)

I walked into the living room where my mother was peacefully seated in front of a nice warm fire with our German Shepard lying at her feet.

Using that maternal radar mothers have, she sensed my real mood despite my smiling face. Knowing I couldn't fool her, I broke down and told her of my frustration in trying to keep up with the frantic pace of my family and how empty I felt after leaving the party for an hour, to discover when I returned that nobody had even noticed that I was gone.

She gave a gentle laugh, leaned back in her chair and told me a story that knocked me out of my socks.

"I know exactly how you feel," she said. "When I was on the road, I traveled with my best friend, Bea Wilson, who was a funnier, prettier and much more talented woman than I was. Every time we went to a party, people just flocked around her and pretty much ignored me."

I shook my head, trying to imagine this woman who was always the center of attention at any gathering being ignored. It seemed an impossible task.

"I'm really having trouble visualizing this, Mom," I said. "Many of my former class-mates with whom I have lost contact still stay in touch with you. My friends that came by, sometimes came just to see you. In fact, two girls have told me that if they could have had you for a mother-in-law, they would have put up with having me as a husband!"

"Well, everything changed for me in one night," she replied. "It was a really big party celebrating the new season. Bea was glorying in her element and as usual, I was off by myself sitting on a couch.

95

"At the other end of the couch sat a young woman who looked lonelier than I felt. I decided that maybe I could make sure there was one less miserable person at the party, so I scooted over and introduced myself. As we talked, she revealed she was a stamp collector and started sharing her experiences. At first, I was uneasy and felt that I was going to be bored and lonely. But as she talked, I became fascinated as she related the countless legends and mysteries associated with stamps. She explained why some stamps were valued in the millions and had me enthralled with tales of some of the great art thefts. The longer she talked, the more people there were who drifted over until she was surrounded by a circle of interested listeners.

"At the end of the evening, as we were all saying goodnights, she hugged me and thanked me for being responsible for the most enjoyable evening of her life.

"Later that night, I couldn't sleep, trying to figure out just what it was I had done. Basically, all I had done was to become sincerely interested in another human being and in doing so, I had changed her life and made the party more enjoyable for everyone. And so, my Darling Son, from that night on, I no longer cared whether anyone ever noticed me. I just made sure I noticed everyone else."

Then with a twinkle in her eye, Mom winked and said, "You know what? I ended up with more dates than Bea."

Hearing that story led me to the discovery that not just physically, but spiritually, I was truly my mother's son. I developed the habit of never letting a day go by without meeting and sincerely appreciating at least one new person.

This simple change in behavior and attitude has brought more blessings and happiness into my life than anything else I have ever done.

Being an active and sincere appreciator had led to creating large successful drama departments, winning speech teams, life-long friendships with former students and the opportunity to be part of the development of teenagers into successful adults, husbands, wives, parents and even now in some cases, grandparents.

My mother's life and teaching made me aware that every human being has tales to be told, experiences that can enrich, insights that can inspire, hobbies that can help, hearts that can heal and laughter that can lighten.

Thank you, Mom. Thank you, on behalf of myself and every student who has ever been inspired by the many Gifts that you, Al, Bob, George, Dad and others like you have left by the Side of the Road.

Basically, all I had done was to become sincerely *interested* in another human being and in doing so, I had changed her life and made the party more enjoyable for everyone.

— Miriam "Bobbie" Schlatter

FOUR HITS AND A MISS

Being kind is one of the simplest hobbies you can develop. Putting on plays and developing successful speech teams is very hard work and demands countless hours of effort. However, the rewards are wonderful. Seeing audiences give kids standing ovations, watching wonderful young people win first place trophies, and years later, hearing them share their memories are rich experiences.

However, some of my happiest moments came from some of my most simple behaviors.

From Boulder, Colorado, a girl (Cathy Keller) wrote me that she was a professional ventriloquist, a career she had embarked upon after seeing me laugh so hard I was crying while watching her recite a comical poem called "Diver Dan." She told me that, up to that point, she had no idea she could be funny.

From Washington, DC, I received copies of articles written by a remarkable young lady (Maura Conlon) who, years before, had written such beautiful poetry that I had her excused from all her classes to share her genius with my students. She said that I was the first adult who made her feel she could write.

One day in class, my students were giving speeches about their heroes when in walked a young man whom I'd had in class four years previously. He told my students I was his hero because after doing a magic act in a talent show when he was in the seventh grade, I had complimented him and asked him to take drama the next year. He said he went home and cried that night because it was the first time someone had invited him to be part of something. Today, Allen Emrich is the publisher of three game magazines and invites thousands of people to annual tournaments he organizes throughout the country.

In 1993, I was speaking at a district conference of student leaders, and a gentleman (Earl Graves) came up to me, shook my hand, and informed me that for 25 years he had been a coach, which was entirely my fault. I asked him how this could be, and he produced a Christmas card I had sent him in 1960. He still had it because it was the first Christmas card he had received from a teacher, a teacher who was coaching football, directing student government and producing plays. Evidently, the fact that someone who was so busy had taken time to wish him a Merry Christmas made him feel very special. Later he thought, "What a great way to spend your life, making young people feel important." So he decided to devote himself to doing the same.

What did I do? I "Enjoyed," I "Invited," I "Sent Good Wishes," and I "Helped" to change the world, four simple civil acts that anyone can do.

I recall my "miss" being a time when I let my ego ruin a special moment for a colleague for whom I had great respect. I feel it well illustrates the need for "humility."

It was his first or second year as a teacher, and he ran up to me to show me a beautiful letter of appreciation he had received from a student. It was easy to see he felt on top of the world. "That's wonderful," I said. "Now be sure to store it in a notebook so you can remember it if ever you get discouraged." (So far, so good but I didn't let it end there because I had to make sure "my" ego got fed.) "I already have many notebooks with letters like this that give me great joy." I could feel the energy flow out of him. "Yea, well..." he muttered as he slowly walked away. In a very subtle, thoughtless way, I had ruined his "moment" in order to glorify myself. It was a most uncivil behavior. The memory haunts me to this day.

Any effort that has *self-glorification*
as its final endpoint
is bound to end in *disaster*.

— Robert M. Pirsig

KNOCKED OFF THE TRACK

Picture a high-powered, supercharged, streamlined train speeding along with a beauty, grace and energy that immediately arrest the attention and admiration of the eye.

Suddenly, there is a loud crashing sound as the majestic machine veers off the track and into a gorge, unable to progress any farther because someone had placed a huge obstacle in its path.

The engine is still filled with fuel and has all of its parts in working order, but it is now stuck because it was knocked "off track."

The same tragedy has befallen countless human beings, people who had discovered their own "special track."

Maybe it was a stage, a woodshop, a basketball court, a computer lab or an orchestra pit. It was a place that made them feel at home.

Life had gone from a dull routine to an exciting adventure. A sense of "purpose" had replaced a feeling of worthlessness.

Success could actually be seen and assured, until the day when that life ran into an obstacle and was "knocked off the track."

Maybe it was just a remark uttered by the thoughtless, the fearful, the jealous, the cruel and the uncivil.

"You're not coordinated enough."

"You call that music?"

"Better people than you have tried that and failed. What makes you think you can do it?"

"Who would want you?"

"Are you really going to wear that face in public?"

Or maybe it was a social snub, a hate-filled argument or a piercing arrow of ridicule.

So the soul that could have soared like an eagle was knocked off track and grounded.

You see we are *all* destined to create happiness. Some of us will make people rejoice because we have walked into a room. Others will cause a celebration because they have walked out of a room.

What causes such uncivil behavior? I believe it is fear. We fear we can't measure up, so we try to protect our egos by sabotaging those who do win.

People seem to have the attitude that says, "no one will notice my dirty shirt so long as nobody with a clean one comes around."

But resentment is like drinking poison and waiting for the other person to die.

Happiness comes from loving people and using things...

Whereas, desperate loneliness comes from loving things and using people...

We always have a choice about what decisions we make when we get "knocked off the track" to get ourselves "back on the track." I believe it has been concisely explained in this quote:

Every *decision* I make is a choice

between a grievance and a miracle.

I let go of grievances.

I choose *miracles*.

— Dr. Deepak Chopra

Throughout our lives, we have seen people with great potential either bury their gifts or turn them into destructive tools to hurt others. History relates facts; myths and legends reveal truth. Maybe the reason that so much of humanity engages in negative behavior is because we have an incorrect view of our true nature.

I would like to introduce you to someone who inhabits my memory and lives in my heart.

THE UGLY DUCKLING

We are all ugly ducklings, and we constantly persecute ourselves for our lack of ability to waddle and quack.

The reason for this problem is not a shortcoming of our own, but it is because in reality we are really SWANS (Souls With A Natural Serenity), and rather than make weird noises and have a comical walk, we are put here to glide on the river of life in such a manner that the entire world is inspired by the gift that we are put here to give.

Sometimes people like Anne Boe come along to reveal people's "Swan-Dom" and remove their "Duck-Hood."

Anne Boe was a genius in the art of networking. She helped many people create successful businesses and life-long friendships through her books, tapes and television appearances on network TV. While receiving a lot of attention, she was great at paying a lot of attention.

Anne Boe created friendships everywhere she traveled. Her legacy is to be found in countless new friendships created by people who followed her advice. We are going to lose, or be lost by everyone we know. Use your mind to photograph the stars in your life. We will never lose Ann because we really got to know her while she was here.

I present the following memorial, which I wrote about her as an illustration of the greatness in our society. Maybe she will remind you of someone you know... or maybe it is *you* who has become the swan!

Remembering Anne Boe

She walked through our lives with wisdom.
She danced in our hearts with delight.
She sang a song of serenity that made us all feel peaceful.
Her listening added life to our existence.
Her humor was so gentle it seemed like a hug.
Her smile made life seem like a toy that we could all enjoy.

The elements of style, grace and integrity were so mixed in her that the entire world could stand up and say this lady was a human being and we thank all the stars in heaven that she passed our way.

The words from *The Other Side of the Mountain* fit best to describe the feelings of those who knew Anne Boe, "How lucky we are to have known someone that to say good-bye is so completely incomprehensible."

(Anne Boe left us April 15, 1996 but will be in our hearts forever) Anne *knew* the "mansions" she left in other people's souls would be her only measure of greatness. She was some kind of architect.

Our death is not an end if we can *live on*

in our children and the younger generation.

For *they are us*, our bodies are only

wilted leaves on the tree of life.

— Albert Einstein

I AM AN APPRECIATOR

My parents are Awareness and Gratitude.
I see the invisible,
I hear the wisdom of the silent,
I encourage life, inspire growth and make miracles.

My grateful heart enriches my senses so that I can...

Look at an acorn and see a tree.
Gaze at a flower and envision a garden.

When I stand in a maternity ward, I look upon new life, a celebration of creativity...

Many souls who have gone before me have been my teachers through their examples...

Like Ben Franklin, who looked at lightning and saw electricity.
William Dawes, who upon discovering a piece of moldy bread
    envisioned penicillin.
Robert Fulton, who discovered that steam was a power
    that could move ships.
Anne Sullivan, who looked beyond appearances when she knew
    that the blind and deaf Helen Keller had vision of the soul...
Winston Churchill, who knew that victory would rise out of the
    ashes of defeat and create The British Empire's Finest Hour...

Like Walt Whitman, I do not speak of miracles; I experience miracles every day, for I know that all of life is a miracle...

To 'appreciate' is to increase value...

The teacher who sees leadership potential in a challenging child, the mother who notices creativity in the inventive child, the father who notices that the stumbling, bumbling youngster has courage...

So many gifts go unnoticed until an Appreciator uses their vision to bless and nourish them... That is my mission: to add to Life through appreciating...

I AM AN APPRECIATOR

The disenfranchised, skeptical and fearful have taken to portraying any assembly of religious people as a "gathering of nuts." So I submit my observations of a church conference where I spoke. The name of the religion is not important because such love is not restricted to one organization, but can be found wherever there is Loving Faith.

THE WORDLESS WELCOME

Long before the ships sailed, trains traveled or planes flew, it was well known that human beings had a built in "sixth sense" radar system... a spiritual sounding board that could sense the atmosphere of any area even before it was entered. When I walked into a meeting one Sunday, I received a multitude of meaningful messages like: "You may call this place your home; Prepare to meet a new family; It's adventure time!" I met more than people. LOVE greeted everyone with hugs and smiles. SPIRIT invented games and danced to music. TRUTH addressed problems and discovered solutions. SOUL revealed the countless unique gifts each individual has to give. JOY made time go by much too quickly. LIFE let everyone know there was energy and victory in every meeting, discussion and plan. FAITH revealed a heroic horizon adorned with dreams of greatness for the youth to whom the torch of civility shall be passed.

It was both inspirational and fun to meet so many people who were attempting the impossible: they were trying to "out-give" life! This caused me to "time travel" with excitement, as it was easy to see a fantastic future ahead for these contributors of charity and higher consciousness.

It was a wonderful holiday from words like "get" and "can't". There was no place for worry, fear, anger and even sleep was considered quite an inconvenience.

So I thank you... you the bearers of the gifts... you messengers of meaning. Being in your presence for the weekend reinvigorated me with the faith that Longfellow discovered when he wrote, "The wrong shall fail, the right prevail and there shall be peace on earth, goodwill to all."

Of course there are many similar groups centered on sports, politics, community service, and hobbies. Look for them, get to know them. If you fly with the eagles, you'll never get stuck gobbling with the turkeys.

A STROLL THROUGH A GRAVEYARD

Sometimes the only things left to remind people of those who have come before are tombstones. Those left behind want others to know that the departed were worthy, heroic, generous, intelligent, etc. I could safely wager that we could travel through the world and not find one marker over a grave that praised the person's possessions.

Could you imagine?

Here Lies Selfish Sam
Born 11-22-47 • Died 4-12-04

He left behind a
New Car • Lots of Money • Plenty of Toys

Bruce Barton wrote about two bodies of water in the Middle East connected by the River Jordan. One is fed by the head waters of the river and opens out into the plains; as it receives, it gives. It is a sea that supports life and civility.

Lovers walk along its banks, children play along its shores, farmers and fishermen gain their livelihood from its gifts. Travelers come from round the world to witness its beauty and hear how miracles were performed. It is called the Sea of Galilee.

The other body of water lies to the South, at the end of the Jordan River. While receiving its contents from the same source, it presents a very different picture. Nothing grows near it or lives in it. Its water has no value, and its stench makes it almost unbearable to be near. You see, it "keeps" every drop it gets. It's called the Dead Sea. It has no civility.

To create more life-giving civility, our culture must do more to acknowledge those who constantly serve; donate blood to the Red Cross; coach Little League and Pop Warner Teams; donate to charities; support churches, synagogues and mosques; donate food and toys to the less fortunate during holiday periods; give freely of their time to hospitals, schools, hospice, scouting and Big Brothers Big Sisters. Our country is filled with these unsung heroes. They fly into our communities with caring civility and keep much of the culture alive.

The universe is so large that if real happiness came from being alone, there is certainly enough room and material for each of us to have our own planet. But without one another, what do we have?

Who will listen to us, teach us, inspire us or receive from us? It is the most simple of truths... WE NEED ONE ANOTHER!

Verna Kelly, an American writer, made an amazing observation when she wrote, "Snowflakes are one of nature's most fragile things. But just look at what they do when they stick together." This is a thought provoking concept, but I do wish to make an addition to it. While they all come together, each snowflake is different; and in joining the whole, they do not surrender their individuality.

A Celebration of Civility's goal is to help create a society where we all work together while appreciating each other's uniqueness. Like the Ancient Greek Pillars, we should join together in supporting a structure, cooperating, not conforming or leaning. Such a world would stand strong for all time like indestructible pyramids of hope.

Civility costs nothing,
and buys *everything*.

— Mary Wortley Montagu

COMMUNICATION

Once I created a speech assignment (which I felt was a great project) and asked my students to relate their most exciting day in school. This was in a very affluent community. My students were way above average and a joy to have in class. Yet, only one third of my charges were able to do the assignment. With all our technology and new tools to use in the classroom, boredom still seems to be a presence of epidemic proportions. May the following fable shed some light.

Like most stories, this tale begins on a nice sunny day.

Like many stories concerning water, this one focuses on a man sitting in a boat in the middle of the lake.

However, this man was not enjoying a peaceful day.

"Stupid Fish!" he thought. "I have put my favorite food on my hook, and they're too dumb to take a bite out of my Twinkies."
And the fish swimming around the hook were undoubtedly thinking, "What's the matter? Did he run out of worms?"

I thought of classrooms where teachers only taught what interested *them* without a moment of consideration for the needs or interests of their students.

I created the following "Self Assessment" for myself as well as for others.

To Be Read Before Each Semester

There is a great deal of distance between loving ourselves and being *in love* with ourselves.

As teachers, we get a lot of attention. In fact, that is part of our job... to be wise, inspiring and funny so that students will pay attention to us.

It naturally follows that the better we become as teachers, the more students listen to us and the more attention we get.

It is at this point that we run into our greatest enemy, an enemy that is invisible and whose name is EGO (Edging Good Out).

It is so easy to forget in the midst of the applause that those students who have given us the "presents" of their attention and appreciation *also* need to be noticed.

"Good" teachers cause students to remember *them*. "Great" teachers help students realize that they *themselves* are worth remembering.

A person all wrapped up in himself makes a very small package. Someone who falls in Love with himself or herself will have no rival.

So we constantly must ask ourselves, "Why are we teaching and for whose benefit?" True, we must use spotlights, but we are here to turn them on *our students*, not ourselves. We are here to teach them "how" to think, not to indoctrinate them as to "what" to think.

Finally, we are not here to impress them with our intelligence, but to help them discover their genius, their Gifts to leave by the Side of the Road.

No person was ever honored for what he received. *Honor* has been the reward for what he *gave*.

— Calvin Coolidge

I AM A COUNSELOR

I Am A Counselor

Young people walk into my office in need of 'answers'...

I have no answers, but I do know where the answers can be found...

Like Dorothy who traveled throughout Oz looking for her Heart's Desire...

And finally discovered it was in her 'own backyard'...

Like the Knights of the Round Table who quested throughout the land in search for the Holy Grail before they realized that the sacred treasure lay in their own souls...

I reveal the inborn greatness that lies within every student I encounter. I encourage them to 'think out loud'...

To express the True Self that lies within each magnificent soul, buried under mounds of criticism...

I am not here to encourage or even inspire but to assist in Discovery...

I do not deal with the students I 'see' but with the greatness they can 'be'...

I encourage them to replace:

> Fear with Faith...
> Doubt with Determination...
> Anger with Appreciation...
> Criticism with Creativity...
> Meanness with Meditation...
> Sound with Silence...
> that which has been Hidden with Hope...

Yes, I am a Counselor who has no answers but has a deep and abiding Faith that Answers DO exist within each searching soul...

I am a Guide to the innate treasures within... Treasures that have Potential to be Powerful Blessings for Humanity...

In the days of the westward movement, pioneers had pathfinders... courageous souls who could discover the shortest and safest ways to arrive at desired destinations and return to guide the way.

Today, we have many people setting off on the adventure of adulthood with no pathfinder to guide them, no idea of where they are going or how to get there. No map, no plan and only the most basic of skills. Often, they were neglected and abused as children and so have no internal compass to guide them. There are those who have gone on the adventure of child rearing who are now lost and wounded, without any idea of how to heal generational legacies of pain with the parenting skills necessary to be loving and effective...

And so it is that we have their children to care for... the children of neglect and abuse.

I AM A CHILD ADVOCATE

I Am A Child Advocate who humbly and knowingly comes to the aide of these children as a volunteer CASA – Court Appointed Special Advocates – and as a volunteer GLA – Guardian Ad Litem – a guardian appointed to represent the interests of a child in litigation. I fervently stay with these children until their cases are closed, guiding them through to safe new lives and into the homes of those Heroes of the Heart ... the Foster Parents and Adoptive Parents.

For many abused and neglected children, I am the one constant adult presence in their lives until they find their permanent homes.

This need speaks deeply to the Advocate's heart, as each year hundreds of thousands of children enter foster care in this country.

Because there are not enough of us to represent all of the children in need, Judges typically assign us their most difficult cases, which we welcome with open arms and hearts.

It is my intention to turn the spot light on our mission. I join with the many ordinary people performing extraordinary miracles in advocating for those children who need us most. ALL are welcome to join and extend our reach exponentially to Heal Today's Children.

We are just a few of the many organizations, passionate individuals and parents who champion the children of today, including those with mental, physical and emotional challenges.

We are all today's courageous souls who know in our hearts that we have been put here to pave the way to the shortest and safest path to arrive at the desired destination: children living, loving, laughing and playing while enjoying safe, healthy and loving homes.

UNION OF EAGLES

Nature is a great teacher. You'll never observe a group of eagles, but you can always see a flock of turkeys.

However, once in awhile, an observer can be treated to a glorious sight... two eagles soaring together while doing a ballet in the sky, a marriage, a union of eagles.

When a storm approaches, a turtle retreats into his shell, a bear seeks the protection of his cave and a rabbit jumps into his hole.

But eagles fly into the rain and clouds, braving the terror of darkness and the ferocity of lightning until they rise above it all and experience a serenity and beauty unknown to the animals below.

When we were young, we believed that the world would welcome us and that people were nice. There was a bunny that hid eggs just for us to find, fairies would leave money under our pillow when we lost a tooth, and a jolly old gentleman would spend his entire life preparing to bring us presents every December. We believed that most people really want us to win, and life is beautiful.

Then comes the day we encounter reality. We come across people who, for some reason, want us to lose and will help us to do so. We discover lies, deceptions, illness, cruelty and death. Then we are told to "grow up" and "face reality," and we are tempted to surrender flight and seek out shells or caves where we can hide.

But there is something within us that causes our hearts to identify with the soul of the eagle. We seek out those few special beings that still hold on to their dreams through faith, and to their loyalties through laughter.

A great marriage or anniversary celebrates the union of eagles, two special people who have challenged the hardships and tragedies of life and have soared beyond the turmoil to the calm of love.

When we see such sights, we feel a little more confident, a little more sure that Love still governs the affairs of humanity. Witnessing the union of eagles can create a highway to the life we have envisioned in our most inspired moments.

Sleep creates a wonderful fantasyland. When we are asleep, nothing is impossible. We can fly into the clouds. We can talk with people who have passed on. We can even play with cartoon characters. Once, I dreamt that I was Zorro, riding across a huge Monopoly board, stealing green houses, and I woke up laughing.

When we wake up, we remain in that fantasy state that believes anything for the next 30 to 45 seconds. Therefore, we have to be very careful how we program ourselves for the day to come. People who say "Good Morning, God" may have a better time than those who say "Good God, It's Morning."

Every morning when you wake up, read the following page to yourself out loud. The words could change your life.

But those who trust in GOD will find new strength.

They will soar high on wings *like eagles*.

They will run and not grow weary.

They will walk and not faint.

— Isaiah 40:31

DAILY RECOMMENDED MOTIVATION

Inside of me, I can feel a seed...it's ME.

It's Me! I'm living, I'm loving, I'm growing and I'm winning. I'm Alive!

Thank God I found out... I am someone... I count... I like me!

Hey World! Look out! I'm growing. I'm giving. I'm free and filled with Power!

Fear may try to speak to me, but that is all it can do.

I just don't listen to fear; I go ahead anyway... I never quit.

There may be times when I'm alone, but I'm never lonely.

I AM A WINNER! I was born a winner, and that which made me a winner is always with me.

Accept me or reject me, for I'm strong enough to stand with power.

If I can like me, so can the world.

I'm Coming! I'm Strong! I'm Me! I am a Winner!

LOOK OUT WORLD! I'M GOING TO MAKE YOU A BETTER, HAPPIER AND MORE PEACEFUL PLACE TO CELEBRATE LIFE!!

In my workshops, I passed this motivation out and challenged students to try it for 30 days and see what would happen. One day, I returned to a school where I had held such a workshop and was greeted by an angry seventh grader.

"I'm so mad at you," he said. "Remember that motivation thing you had us read? Well I did it for 17 days!"

"Why are you mad at me?" I asked

"Because now I'm so excited I can't sleep. The other day, I cleaned my room without being told to, and my Mom thinks I'm up to something!"

After a good laugh, I called his mother and we had a great talk. Eventually, you will write your own challenge. As the body needs vitamins like A, B, C and all the others, so the mind needs the Mental Vitamins of positive energy.

Have you ever wondered what an American looks like? We are the first people not born of blood, but spirit.

In the words of F. Scott Fitzgerald, "France was a land, England was a people but America was an idea." What a great idea!

THE UNSEEN CEREMONIES

"Why are we here, Daddy?"

"To celebrate the memory of a great man who saved our part of the country from poverty, my son."

"How did he do that, my Father?"

"When our ancestors who had enslaved his ancestors were facing financial ruin, this man created over 400 products that we could grow, use and sell from a peanut."

And so the white family bowed their heads before the monument, remembering Dr. George Washington Carver.

"Why are we here, Daddy?"

"To celebrate the memory of those men who gave their lives so our people could be free."

"How did they do that, my Father?"

"They fought a Civil War to destroy a system that their ancestors had employed to enslave our ancestors."

So the black family bowed their heads before the monuments, remembering the sacrifices of Civil War Veterans.

It has taken us centuries, and will still take far more time for us to make the long march from warring tribes, races and nations to the realization that, despite so many apparent differences, we are still running in the same race... The Human Race.

"It is only with the heart that one sees clearly —what is essential is invisible to the naked eye." —the Fox in The Little Prince

BIG BROTHERS BIG SISTERS

We do what we do because we have hearts that 'see' what others miss. Where they see problems... we see potential.

We see life in the listless and a great capacity for love in the lonely. We see potential victory in those who think of themselves as victims... We see the power to stand tall in those who have fallen.

We fight for the lives of youth who feel they only exist... Our weapons are humor, hugs and hope.

We transform negativity, hatred, prejudice and cynicism as we are there for those who need us.

We joyfully participate in their growth and open their eyes to the gifts they have to give, so they will come to know they have value beyond their wildest dreams...

We get to be:

Architects helping to build lives filled with joy, hope and pride;
Doctors healing hurt feelings and restoring shattered dreams;
Statesmen giving others the confidence to govern themselves;
Explorers, discovering continents of potential in each child;
Lawyers making a case for receiving through contributing;
Entertainers creating excitement over the progress of the human spirit through the ages;
Coaches giving guidance in how to win the game of life;
Teachers instructing humanity in the art of respecting themselves and each other.

We are Big Brothers Big Sisters ...
We choose to be loving members of The Family of Humanity.

I AM A 4-H'ER

I am a proud and grateful 4-H'er, an advocate and appreciator of life. I don't just believe in miracles, I have witnessed them take place daily in nature. I have planted seeds to grow into gardens, acorns into forests and put pairs of animals together that develop into herds and flocks. The animals I love have taught me more than I could have ever hoped to have learned from a textbook.

I study how to prepare meals, create clothing fashions and bring warmth to a home. Through understanding and believing in potential, I inspire others to reach new levels of success.

When birds protect their young with their wings, and horses run with their colts, and eagles insist that their off-spring learn to fly, we come to understand the confidence and abilities that can be created by committed and loving leadership.

While joyfully receiving the gifts of eggs, milk and vegetables, I seek to give back through nurturing and cultivating life. Using what I harvest from the earth, I create magic in the kitchen.

Through my love and attention, I can turn my livestock into champions which I parade as judges grade their magnificence.

Science has taught me that, for growth to take place, harmony must be created. I have learned to lead by listening to those who follow.

I learn how to positively participate in government. I promote cooperation and teamwork while at the same time endorsing individuality. I and my fellow 4-H'ers represent all races, religions and cultures, and as we work and build together, we often discover we have become families.

Our HEADS inspire us to offer our HANDS in HEARTfelt friendship to all who live on this earth with the goal of being the leaders of tomorrow creating a HEALTHier world.

The 4-H Clover symbolizes four actions which 4-H members strive to accomplish. The four H's stand for: Head, Hands, Heart, and Health, as it is in my pledge.

I Pledge:
My Head to clearer thinking,
My Heart to greater loyalty,
My Hands to larger service and
My Health to better living for my Club,
    my Community, my Country and my World.

I AM A SCOUT

My ancestors sought to conquer the wilderness... I have learned to be nature's friend and student.

Through facing new challenges every day, we develop strength, discover new abilities and strengthen the bonds of friendship.

I wear my badges on my uniform, but more importantly I wear the lessons learned while earning those badges in my mind, heart and soul...

My companions are of different races, cultures and religions, yet we are a unified family as we face challenges, build communities and follow dreams...

I care for those who face hardships and handicaps, but I see no poor people... for to me every human being is rich in potential, and I am dedicated to helping them express their greatness.

There is a price to be paid when walking the high road...

I have never pursued popularity but have been devoted to principle... I have great hope for humanity, as I am a student of life.

Nature teaches me the power of re-birth and the wisdom to be found in walking one's own path...

I know that all people are potential gifts of friendship, that challenge creates character, that laughter helps to love life and that I stand at my tallest when I reach down to help a fallen human being...

My scouting has taught me that life is an uphill journey but with each step the view becomes more beautiful...

During the times of exploration, a 'scout' was the one who went ahead into uncharted territory to blaze a path...

Today we are trained to look for 'potential' in problems, 'dreams' in danger, 'laughter' in love and 'faith' in humanity even when human frailty is the most visible...

I am a Scout who learns from the past, plans for the future and joyfully lives TODAY...

Boy Scout Oath:
Duty to God and country, Duty to other people and Duty to self.

Girl Scout Promise:
On my honor, I will try to serve God and my country, to help people at all times and to live by the Girl Scout Law.

The world is so full of wonderful, giving people we may never meet, people who help us get through our day, people who protect us.

I AM YOUR BADGE

As long as I exist, there will be civilization.

Your life will be longer because I am willing to risk my life being shorter.

Before every criminal I arrest can be judged guilty, I must be proven to be just.

If one of my brother officers commits an act of cruelty, it is seen throughout the entire world, while the countless kind and heroic deeds remain the best-kept secrets on earth.

Along with traffic control, crime prevention and mystery solving, I have also...

Talked to your children in school,

Pulled you out of burning buildings and wrecked cars,

Helped your babies be born with only a squad car for a delivery room,

Supported charities, coached little league teams and ushered at mosques, churches and synagogues.

I belong to the roll call for the ages.

My name appears alongside:

The Centurions of Rome,

The Knights of the Round Table,

The Minutemen of Lexington and Concord.

The strain I have endured has created problems in personal relationships.

The danger I face has often cost me health and even, in some cases, life itself.

At times, it seems that the authority I carry has created more fear and hatred than trust and appreciation from the people I protect.

There are times I ask myself, "Why? Why do I do it?"

Then I see children playing in their front yard, teenagers dressed in formal attire to celebrate a forthcoming graduation, a husband and wife moving into their first home, and an elderly couple holding hands while taking a walk at twilight, all in relative safety and security. When I see such sights, I know, I know...

IF WE WILL ONLY LOOK TWICE

Adie Shickelgruber was a young Austrian living in Germany. With all of his heart, he wanted to be a painter. He could paint buildings and "still life." His shadows were very strong, and his sense of color coordination was not half bad, but he couldn't paint people. He was unable to get fluidity in his work. He applied to three art schools and was not only turned down, but was greeted with ridicule and treated with contempt. He received no encouragement and finally surrendered his dream in favor of politics. He did away with his name, as it was too long to fit on a ballot. His new name, Adolf Hitler, not only fit on the ballot, but to make things easier, he eventually did away with the entire ballot!

Think about it. One compassionate, dedicated art teacher could have saved us from World War II. I believe with all my heart that that person was alive but did not fulfill his or her destiny for being on the planet.

In the mid '80s, a young man arrived at our school, having just moved from the Midwest to California.

Needless to say, the culture shock was intense.

Think back to your days in Junior High. I am sure you will recall how all the social groups were well established and tight by mid term.

Henry was a soccer player, but all the teams had been formed. So, being thrown into a new life style where new people were not openly welcomed and being unable to participate in his favorite sport, Henry was fast descending into a deepening depression

His parents, wishing to cheer him up, took him shopping for new clothes. Now, in Henry's community back home, all the boys had yellow sweat suits. So his parents picked him out a brand new one.

The kids at our school had never seen a yellow sweat suit, so when Henry got out of his parents car in front of the school, he was greeted with ridicule and name calling. Three girls especially led the parade of put downs, and made up some scathing nick names.

After my third period preparation class, I was walking toward my car, when Henry stormed out of his classroom and almost ran into me. I saw the mixture of anger and terror in his eyes. Grabbing him by the arm, I asked where he was going.

"Let me go, Mr. Schlatter, I mean it!" he shouted.

Letting him go anywhere at that moment would probably have been the worst possible thing to do. I almost carried him to the counselor's office, where two wise counselors quickly sized up the situation. Within one hour we had him in a special hospital for suicide prevention. Before his encounter with me, he was on his way to throw himself onto the freeway that ran by our school.

Whether it is directing a frustrated painter from becoming a worldwide despot or stopping a young boy from killing himself, we need to *always* act with caring civility.

Let me neglect no *kindness*

for I may never pass this way again.

— Said in many different ways
by many great thinkers

Have you ever noticed that no matter how many despots we destroy,
a new one always rises to take his place? Maybe there's another way...

THE DESTROYED ENEMY

"Don't you remember that vicious thing he did to you?"

"No," Clara Barton replied, "But I *do* distinctly remember forgetting it."

You will never get ahead by trying to get even. Revenge cheats us out of many potential blessings.

Before the Civil War it was illegal to teach a slave how to read and write, yet from these ashes of prejudice there arose a man who saved the economic livelihood of the former oppressors. As the cotton market was beginning to subside, Dr. George Washington Carver discovered hundreds of uses for the lowly peanut and re-energized the Southern economy. How many potential Carvers who might have given great gifts in medicine, literature, invention, entertainment and social innovations were suppressed by such cruelty as enforced ignorance?

In the late '60s, at a high school where I was teaching, I encountered a young man who used his size to intimidate others. His meanness was legendary. I saw students change their direction just to avoid him. Oh, he got his applause from the shallow and the conformists. But he received friendship from no one.

This true story has a moral that is self-evident.

Marshall was a person who made everyone happy when he would leave a room. He was one of the earliest advocates of the "put down" humor of today. He sneered at everything and ridiculed everyone. He was just as cruel physically, shoving people, "accidentally" stepping on toes, always with just enough self-restraint to stay out of official trouble.

Dennis was an extremely hard working student, staying in the library till closing and always ready to help anyone who needed extra coaching.

So it was that Marshall chose Dennis for his particular wrath, once even "accidentally" breaking his glasses.

Many of us tried to straighten Marshall out, but to no avail. I must admit that he was one of a handful of students that I could not bring myself to like. In fact, it was just the opposite. I am ashamed to admit I intensely *disliked* him. I just knew Will Rogers had never met Marshall.

Finally, the day came that Marshall stepped over the line once too often, and he was expelled.

Years later, I was invited to the 20th reunion of Dennis' class. It was great to see so many of my former students who had developed into such successful adults.

Then came one of the greatest shocks I ever received in my 30 years of teaching. Seated together in one booth with their wives were Dennis and Marshall.

My curiosity compelled me to walk over and say hello... and find out just how such an unusual pairing had developed.

After exchanging greetings and noticing a warmth and kindness in Marshall's bearing I would have thought impossible years ago, I commented that I never expected to see the two of them hanging out together.

"Hang out?" Marshall said. "Dennis has grown into more my brother than if we had shared the same parents. You see, Mr. Schlatter, you can learn an awful lot about being a human being when the person whose life you made miserable in high school turns out to be the only doctor in town who has learned a special operating procedure that saves your son's life."

It is foolish to war against potential allies.

That so-called "dumb jock" may become the policeman who stops burglars from robbing your house.

The one you call "that air-headed cheerleader" may become the recreation leader who develops a program that gives your children hours of enjoyment and the opportunity to discover new talents.

The fellow you have labeled an "intellectual snob" may grow into the statesman who helps to solve a governmental crisis and saves you large amounts of money you had invested or would have been taxed.

If one drives into the small town of Ramona, California, in the early morning, there are places where you turn right into the sun and even with the visor down, you are totally blinded to the road for 10 to 15 yards. Hundreds of people travel this road every day, and yet there is seldom an accident because, if you look down from the sun, you see a double yellow line in the middle of the road. All one has to do is stay to the right of that line to drive in safety. Now that line was probably painted during the heat of the day by an unknown laborer, yet his humble work saves lives every minute of the morning. Is he not invaluable? Is he not deserving of our consideration?

How do we know that the person we cut off on the freeway or push out of the way in a grocery line is not that very same "life saver?"

When you hold *resentment* toward another,

you are bound to that person or condition by

an emotional link that is stronger than steel.

Forgiveness is the only way to

dissolve that link and get free.

— Catherine Ponder

The most misrepresented profession in our popular culture is that of the businessman. Yet the ability to do charitable works depends on the success of these creators of wealth. I would now like to tell the story of such a man.

KINDNESS CREATES CUSTOMERS

Henry Ford was truly one of the most controversial Americans to ever walk across our national stage.

However, it should be pointed out that he became one of the wealthiest people of all time through a simple act of kindness.

At the beginning of the twentieth century, there was a lot less money, but it could buy a whole lot more. A very nice house cost about $5,000. You could support yourself on $10 per week. Steak dinners cost 29 cents.

Most of Ford's employees earned about $1 a day. One day, the idea occurred to him that his own workers would make good customers, but to "buy," one has to have "money" to spend.

So, Ford amazed the nation by raising salaries in his plants to an average of $5 per day.

Such generosity from an employer was unheard of. How would you feel if your boss raised your salary five times over?

Once again, the pillars of Civility began to rise in unison. Whatever his motive, Mr. Ford's action did have a great deal of kindness in it. Seeing their boss act with such integrity, the people in the plants became very appreciative and totally committed to the Ford Motor Company. Now that they were members of the middle class, all those laborers could afford automobiles. And when someone mentioned automobiles to those people, only one name glared in front of them. FORD!

It seems to be an unwritten law that you can't out-give life. Truly the more you give, the more you live.

We see countless protest demonstrations in favor of job rights, gun rights, civil rights, and that is the way a democracy is supposed to function. However, it seems that, as a society, we think that we can be happy only after "other people" give us what we feel we deserve, and we forget the truly great rights we can give to ourselves. As I reread the Bill of Rights for Teenagers *that I shared earlier, I realized that everyone needs to consider and enjoy a personal Bill of Rights.*

NEW BILL OF RIGHTS

I have the right to own my own broadcasting network, produced in the studio of my mind, with film at the visualization hour.

I have the right to develop the qualities I most want in my soul mate, and thus to attract that person into my own life.

I have the right to be a greater adventurer than history has ever recorded, to explore the continent of my mind and to discover the islands of my new talent, interests and joys.

I have the right to praise my accomplishments and abilities instead of cursing my faults and mistakes.

I have the right to learn the lesson of the eagle and know that being alone does not mean being lonely—and that the greatest way to overcome a storm is to fly into it and above it to the peaceful heaven that comes with victory.

I have the right to turn off my television set and sleep no more than necessary, so I will never be confused with one of the walking dead.

I have the right to do more than the work to which I am assigned, and thus make myself indispensable wherever I am.

I have the right to play and laugh and enjoy and grow with my family, and thus create a sanctuary for the heart where I am always welcome, always understood, always appreciated and my higher self is always seen.

I have the right to exercise my body and feed it the best of foods so that my mind and spirit are carried in the most attractive of carriages.

I have the right to run with the deer, to swim with the dolphins, and to fly with the eagle, so I will never have to flock with the turkeys.

I have the right to develop my relationship with that power greater than I am and thus establish my identity on the rock of eternity for all time.

If you still doubt your worthiness, the following story might help.

THE INSPIRATIONAL HAMBURGER

It was 1971. I had left the teaching profession, only to discover how much I loved it and desperately wanted to return, but I was facing a brick wall. This was a time when school districts were laying teachers off, not hiring them, and those that were being hired were in the fields of math and science, certainly not drama. Also, because I had taught for a number of years, it would be more expensive to hire me than a new teacher straight out of college. The school where I wanted to resume my teaching career was the most popular school in the district with great kids and a fantastic Principal, Edward J. Austin. I had been a fool. I hadn't appreciated how great my profession was. In business, I had been a total washout. If there was a bad investment, I could find it. In fact, I was thinking about writing an autobiography with the title, *Gullible Travels*.

So, there I was in Bob's Big Boy Restaurant, unemployed, almost broke and unable to blame anybody by myself.

As I approached the cashier to pay my check, a wonderful thought occurred to me. My hamburger was being digested. It was being turned into skin, bone, blood, nerve fiber, hair and eyes, and I had nothing to do with it. If I had a billion dollars, I couldn't build a laboratory or hire enough scientists to do what was being done inside my body for free. Then I realized that my heart was being made to beat by this same invisible power. It was like life saying, "I haven't condemned you. I will continue to fill you with energy and miracles no matter how many mistakes you make." I walked out into a new day thinking "God loves me." I may not have deserved it, but that didn't make any difference to this universal power. I knew I was blessed and destined for success.

Soon thereafter, I was unexpectedly hired by Mr. Austin at the school I desired with full pay and six drama classes, which began 20 wonderful years in Los Alamitos.

Every theater group has a name, and to be true to my discovery, even though it might have irritated some people, I had to call our company ... *God Love Ya Productions*.

I could fill a book with the letters from graduates who told how, at different times in their lives, within each of their hearts they were reminded that the power that created them also constantly loved them ... every second of the day.

I Am A Hospice and Home Care Giver

I believe in life, which is why I deal with the experience called death. I am like a conductor who gives guidance to those about to board the train to eternity.

My experiences have taught me that bodies die but love and memories live forever.

My comrades in hospice and home care are earth angels. They move among the suffering, tickling funny bones, lightening emotional loads and creating new visions of life.

As my patients stand on the stage before the final act, temporary problems seem to fade while love, gratitude, forgiveness, hope and joy begin to glow with celestial light.

Many of the people I have sought to comfort have seen their hearts grow to heroic proportions. They walk arm in arm through the valleys of grief and memories of good times, while thoughts of appreciation are given voice.

I have come to believe that, as one's existence on this plane seems more tenuous, an awareness of a larger life that is to follow becomes stronger.

Finally, when the curtain has fallen, with tears in my eyes and a smile in my heart, I leave to go to the next place I am needed with the knowledge that the only thing that has died is death itself.

We are not human beings on a spiritual journey.

We are *spiritual beings* on a human journey.

— Stephen R. Covey

SOME GUESTS LEAVE NO NAME, JUST A MEMORY

This story involves a dedicated teacher, a visitor and a movie.

She stands 5 feet, 4 inches tall, but when it comes to inspiring students, filling a classroom with joy and confidence, motivating children and helping fellow staff members to reach beyond their grasp, Paula Worsham is a tall tower of talent (or a GIANT).

While revealing to students their potential to reach for the stars, she has always had her feet planted firmly on the ground.

Her relationship with her God has been too personal to ever be hampered by the dogma of any particular religion. Although tremendously spiritual, she doesn't have a superstitious bone in her body.

Now that you have met my friend, Paula Worsham, you will all the more appreciate the gift she gave me on January 30, 1994.

We met in a neighborhood restaurant to discuss the grades her students had earned during the time I had been her substitute. My presence in her classroom for a month had been necessitated by her need to have a doctor-advised operation.

While we talked, I was amazed how someone who had just had serious surgery could seem so excitedly alive and yet so peacefully centered.

I had loaned her a copy of my favorite movie of 1993, *Heart and Souls*, an uplifting story of four guardian angels.

"So, did you love it?" I asked.

"Oh yes," she replied, "especially after meeting my new friend."

"Your new friend?" I queried.

"Well, I'll try to tell you about it," she said, as her eyes started to fill with tears.

I leaned forward in concentrated and shocked amazement. Her experience in working with juvenile delinquents and her mid-western culture had made Paula one tough lady, so "tears" were something that I had only seen once before during our 20 years of friendship.

She then proceeded to give me an "experience" wrapped gift, and I pass it on to you.

When she awoke in the recovery room, a nurse with the most radiant and warmest smile she had ever seen greeted her. "No matter what they tell you," the nurse said, "don't you worry."

In her peppy way, Paula smiled and sleepily replied, "OK," and drifted back to sleep.

The next morning, she was visited by her doctor, who told her the operation was a success, but they had discovered something they didn't like and would have to run some tests to make sure it wasn't cancer.

After he left, she lay there filled with anxiety. She didn't fear death, but she worried about her husband and her family and also her students, with whom she was enjoying such a great and productive year. "Oh, not now," she prayed, "not when I have so much to do." But then, the face of that nurse appeared in her consciousness and she again heard the words, "Don't you worry." She felt at ease and comforted.

The next day, after the tests, she was returned to her room. Judy, her favorite nurse, came in and asked if there was anything she could do for Paula.

"Yes, I'd really like some orange juice."

"Right away," said Judy as she left the room.

Paula lay there with countless conflicting thoughts rushing through her mind. She looked over toward the door and there stood the nurse she had seen in the recovery room.

"Oh, hi!" said Paula.

"I just came by to tell you you're perfectly fine, and you will have time to make all your dreams come true."

"Thank you," Paula said. "Can you come in and visit while I wait for my test results?"

"No, I won't be able to do that," the nurse replied. "I'm needed elsewhere. Much happiness to you."

Upon saying that, the nurse walked away.

A few seconds later, Judy walked in with the orange juice.

"Judy, who is that nurse? What's her name? She sure knows how to remove worry," Paula asked.

"What nurse?" asked Judy.

"Why, you must have seen her. She just left."

"Paula, I just came down the hallway. If anyone had left your room, I would have seen her."

Just then, Paula's husband, Paul, came in with flowers and a big smile. "I just heard everything's perfect," he said.

"Who told you, Paul?" asked Paula.

"Why, a nurse who greeted me as I got off the elevator. She must have seen me here yesterday, because she knew I was your husband and she told me all was well."

"What did she look like, Paul?"

Paul then described the nurse who had just left the room.

"We don't have any nurse working on this floor who fits that description," Judy said.

Paula put her head back on the pillow and started laughing as Paul and Judy looked at each other in total confusion.

Needless to say, all the tests came back and "there was nothing to worry about."

Paula and Paul went on to enjoy their new house, and Paula continued to be a blessing to her students, right up to June 2000 when she finally retired.

I leave to you, my unseen friends, to draw your own conclusions as to who Paula's mysterious visitor really was.

All I can tell you is that, as you read my description of her, you'll know why I believe everything happened just as she said.

Was the nurse a special aide in the hospital who had privileged information or was she "something else?" One thing we can know for sure, Paula was visited by kindness, a kindness only the "kind" can understand, either by someone else or... you decide.

Yesterday is but a *Dream*,

Tomorrow is only a *Vision*,

but *Today*, well lived, makes every

Yesterday a Dream of *Happiness*

and every Tomorrow a Vision of *Hope*,

Therefore Look To *This Day*...

— Old Saying

Like Paula, my father was a "no nonsense" person. A complete American with German traditions and self-discipline, he was a tremendous role model. His story deserves to be coupled with Paula's.

THE INVISIBLE GUEST

Dad always wanted to be a doctor. He was even a medic in World War I. But my grandfather insisted he become an engineer. Not wanting to rebel against his father but still following his own dream, Dad carried a double major in engineering and medical science.

One day, his grades arrived home before he did, and my Grandfather, anxious to see his son's progress, had opened the envelope and became aware of Dad's plans.

When Dad arrived home, he was greeted by one irate Father.

"How dare you disobey me!" my grandfather shouted as he slapped my Dad hard across the face.

Dad left home that day, never to return. Shortly thereafter, he went to war, leaving my Mother, with whom he was deeply in love. My aunts did not like my mother, to whom my father had been devoted since they were nine years old. When Dad was in the service, they wrote him that she had married someone else (which was a lie).

Upon getting out of the service, Dad went to Chicago to begin his tremendous career as a great salesman.

During this time, my mother was touring throughout the United States with her violin, not knowing why Dad had quit writing her. One day, while she was eating lunch in a restaurant, a man walked past her table and, with his left hand, straightened his hair.

Years before, Dad had broken his little finger on his left hand, and it had never totally straightened... and this is what my Mother noticed in this man walking by her.

"George!" she yelled. The man turned around, and, sure enough, it was Dad. Upon hearing that Mom had never married, he wasted no time. They were joined together within two weeks.

Their life was so filled with love that Dad was even able to re-establish communication with my Grandfather. They developed a cordial relationship, but were never as close as they had been up to that fateful day when the grades were discovered.

A few years later, Grandfather Schlatter passed away, and Dad was left with a void in his heart that he felt would never heal.

My parents didn't like Christmas; they loved Christmas. Following a tradition established by Grandfather Schlatter, they waited to put up the tree and put out the presents until Christmas Eve when we were asleep. So we grew up thinking Santa not only delivered gifts, but he also put up and decorated our Christmas trees.

One Christmas Eve, when my brothers were still small and I was not yet born, Mom and Dad had finished their fun filled chores and were peaceably sitting in front of the fire, looking at the twinkling tree and watching the snow peacefully fall outside. Dad's thoughts drifted to my Grandfather. "Just as you did for us, Dad, we have done for our boys," he thought to himself. He was filled with an intense wish and/or prayer that they could have re-established the warmth that had at one time been in their relationship before my grandfather's departure.

Silent Night, which was always Grandfather Schlatter's favorite Christmas Carol, came on the radio, and suddenly the big front door in the living room, which had definitely been shut to keep out the Midwestern cold, opened. At that moment, all my Dad's thoughts about his Father became very peaceful. He and Mom sat very still, captivated by an atmosphere they could not explain. All my Dad knew was that any pain he had felt about Granddad had left, never to return. In its place was a feeling of comforting love and forgiveness.

My brother George was a sleepwalker who would wake up where he had been led in his unconscious state.

The next morning Mom and Dad asked George if he had been sleepwalking the previous night.

"No," replied George, "but I did have the strangest dream that a very important guest had come to see us, and I had to go downstairs to let him in."

Love knows no time or space.
Love never dies.
People's bodies die, but love remains.
Love even comes after Death to heal and to Create great holidays — which is another lesson taught by the greatest teacher of all... LIFE!

Dear Becky,
I wish you always the feeling of comforting love. You are a gentle & kind Spirit that is growing & growing stronger - you give your strength to others because love and love allows no boundries faith because of your knowing. I am richer by knowing you.
Love,
Andrew

133

Some of my father's greatest teachings were not through words but through fun traditions.

THE CHRISTMAS CONTRACT

During our early youth, our father established a wonderful but somewhat painful Christmas tradition.

To understand the total impact this game had, you must understand that our father had many outstanding qualities. But the most important one was Integrity.

I can't remember him ever breaking a promise. So you can imagine our excitement when he announced it was time for us to make a list of the presents we desired. He even supplied the paper (lots of it, by the way) and the pencils.

With total sincerity, he said, "Whatever you want, boys. Don't hold back." And we knew he meant it. Like I said earlier, we had learned that his word was as good as gold.

So with great enthusiasm we began this most exciting and pleasurable task. Among many other things, each list contained a pony, a high-powered rifle and so on.

Now, there was one catch... there was the "contract."

The contract was the understanding that any acts of mischief, broken furniture and/or windows, undone chores, grades below a "B" or ignored curfews would cause one request to be removed from the list.

Oh, and we made out the list on the first day of September.

By the September 3rd, the pony had been removed from every list. Shortly thereafter, the high-powered rifles followed. It was a great tradition that created a lot of laughs and enjoyment as we related the story to various guests, girlfriends, future wives and grandchildren.

But it was not until I was in my 20s that I discovered the lesson behind the tradition. Dad was teaching us to dream big, that no goal was beyond our reach, *if only we would pay the price.*

And you know something, dear reader. I firmly believe with all of my heart that if we had truly behaved for those four months, on Christmas morning there would have been four ponies standing in the back yard.

The following stories relate how some of the greatest teachers I have ever known taught me how to be a better teacher.

LOOK FOR THE RIGHT SEED

In between my years at Katella High School and Oak Junior High School, I spent a year traveling and taking assignments as a long term substitute for teachers who were going to be absent for two or three weeks for a variety of reasons.

One class to which I was assigned was at a school that was so tough that the chess team was on steroids! (I'm just kidding, but it seemed like it!) The teacher I was replacing had "sold out" in order to avoid conflict. He had made a deal with the kids that if they would do three math problems per day, they could then talk or play games the rest of the period. You can just imagine their attitude when I took over in mid May and gave them a full day's workload and passed out an "F" to each of those who only did three problems instead of the assigned 20.

On my second day in this class, I was subjected to a chorus of complaints, and very creative insults.

After hearing such endearing comments as...

"What'd you do? Leave your brains in your other pants?"

"Your an idiot, what makes you think you can take away our freedom?"

"Hey, Schlatter, when do you Nazi's meet?"

"If you fell on your butt, I bet you'd need brain surgery."

By the end of the day, I was in shell shock. In one 45-minute period, I had heard more insults than I had in my entire career up to that point. Having taught drama, sponsored student government, and done some coaching, I was used to an entirely different type of student. I had never encountered an entire room filled with anger, depression and defeatism.

I felt like a tennis player who had suddenly been thrown into a rugby match without even knowing the rules.

All sorts of thoughts crossed my mind that night.

"Did the prisons know that all these young ruffians were free?"

"Maybe there *was* a Dr. Frankenstein and he had children, all of them in this town."

I had no idea where to start. It seemed so hopeless. Their anger and apathy seemed to be insurmountable barriers. How could I help them overcome lifelong habits of failure in only three weeks?

I went for a walk that evening at twilight. I just sort of wandered, lost in my confusion and despair. Suddenly, I came across the most beautiful flowerbed I had ever seen. I stood there transfixed by this most glorious display of total beauty.

Then I started to wonder, "What are flowers made out of anyway?"

Books are made out of paper and cardboard.

Cakes are the result of mixing flour, eggs, milk, sugar, baking soda, flavoring and so on.

But what goes into a flower?

Then I looked at the "dirt," that horrible brown stuff we don't want to get on our clothes and we immediately wash off our hands.

However, if the right seed comes in contact with that unwanted substance, it would blossom into a rainbow of colors. I wondered, "Maybe that's what so many human beings are like, feeling worthless, but actually just waiting for the right seed to come along and be planted."

The next day, I began class in the following manner.

"Take out your text books."

"*Grumble #&% & Grumble*" was the immediate response.

"Now put them under your desks."

"Huh?????"

"Now put all the chairs in a circle."

"This is getting weird, man."

I then asked each student to tell me things they liked. It took a while to get started but eventually, they began to enjoy telling about their favorite activities. (Naturally, I had to censor some stories about various activities before they even got started.)

We did no actual work that day or the next. The rest of the week was spent enjoying and listening to each other. A little bit of trust slowly built to a point where the kids started to share their dreams or secret goals.

Needless to say, the kids loved it because, from their point of view, they didn't have to do any work. But, I had a secret plan. Once we got them thinking in terms of lifetime goals, I was able to inquire what they would need to fulfill these priceless plans. In a very strange way, the need for math kept popping up. Some (not all, not even a majority) started asking for some math instruction to help them catch up.

After a week and a half, we were back at the math books with a new attitude.

Because we planted some seeds of hope, civility, kindness, courtesy and appreciation, I was blessed to witness them blossom with new interest and enthusiasm. Like the dirt, everyone has the potential to come forth with blossoms of talent.

The power of connection is played out through
how we *label* a child, and then is transmitted
directly to the child through our *attitudes*.
When we get in touch with our own attitudes,
beliefs and resistance about any challenging situation we may
be dealing with, we, ourselves, will be *transformed*.
And when we are personally transformed,
we set new energy in motion that will *instantaneously*
affect the lives of those children in our care.

— Mary Robinson Reynolds

You also have the right to look for creative new ways to handle old challenges...

NEVER DO HOMEWORK, DO HOME PLAY

Geometry and I were not good friends. In fact, the way it put me in "D" land, I felt we were mortal enemies.

Fortunately, I had a teacher, Mr. Bloch, who taught "students" as well as subjects.

One day, after returning a test paper which featured a "one-legged A," he asked me to stay after class.

"You don't care much for math do you," he said, leaning back in his chair while giving me a kindly but challenging gaze over his glasses.

"No, Sir," I replied, "it seems like a foreign language I'll never learn to speak."

"But you do like murder mysteries?" he asked with a sly grin. You see, Mr. Bloch had taken time to know each one of us personally. During one of our discussions, he had learned that I loved Sherlock Holmes novels.

"How long does it take you to read an entire mystery?" he asked.

"Once I get into it, I seldom put it down until I've finished it. I just can't wait to find out who did it."

"Okay then," he said as he jumped out of his chair. "I don't want you to do any more geometry."

"Wow! I'll buy into that!" I said with a big smile.

"I want you to solve murder mysteries!"

"What?" I asked, totally confused.

"Let me show you what I mean." He took out a blank piece of paper and drew a weirdly shaped triangle. Pointing to it, he said, "There's your mystery. Now I'll give you two clues. One angle is 35 degrees, and the other is 30 degrees. Now the third angle is the murderer. How many degrees does *it* have?"

One of the few things I had learned was that a triangle had 90 degrees. "25 degrees," I answered.

"Good! You caught him. Now put him in jail."

"Where's jail?" I asked.

"On the paper," he bellowed. "Do no more math problems. Solve mysteries."

Something caused me to catch his vision, and that night, for the first time, I started my geometry homework first. I was shocked to discover how much fun it could be using Mr. Bloch's approach. Eventually, I even bought a cheap curved-stem pipe to chew on while I "attacked" the "mysteries" ala my hero, Sherlock Holmes. By the end of the semester, I was shocked to discover I had a "B+."

At that time, I had no idea I was going to be a teacher. But the lesson stayed with me. Mr. Bloch taught me two important things that day. My brother, Bob, often repeated the first thing.

"Never do anything you don't like to do... just learn to like what has to be done."

Years later, his method of teaching students along with teaching subjects came back to my memory when I myself became a teacher.

One day, in 1977, the Principal called me in and asked me to teach a geography class along with my drama classes. Chuck Darrington was a great educator that I would never let down.

There was just one problem... I HATED GEOGRAPHY!

But then, in my imagination, I saw Mr. Bloch's smiling face, and I thought, yes, I hate geography, BUT I love jokes. So, I turned it into a joke class with observations such as...

"Women hate Eurasia. They say, that's not I Asia, that's *Your* Asia. The mountains there are a bunch of male chauvinists because they're all *Him*alayas. There's not one *Her*alaya in the bunch."

"A tundra where there are no trees or shrubberies is bad news for Bambi and Rin Tin Tin."

"A peninsula is a piece of land that told a lie like Pinocchio, and that's why it stretched out into the ocean."

"The Prime Meridian is the part of the earth that is cooked best."

Corny? You bet! But the kids loved repeating what their crazy geography teacher had said, but (and here's the sneaky part) in order to repeat the jokes, they had to learn the geography. My class came in third among seventh grade geography classes in the district that year.

Yes, Mr. Bloch knew math backwards and forwards. But he LEARNED his students. Such a kindness had a lasting effect on my life and eventually the lives of my students.

Thank you, Mr. Bloch. Thank you for teaching me to teach before I even knew that I wanted to be a teacher.

A CELEBRATION OF CIVILITY
IN THE CLASSROOM

A popular cartoon among educators portrays a teacher talking to a group of parents at an Open House. In this cartoon, the teacher is saying, "Let's make a deal. If you promise not to believe all the stories you hear about what goes on in this classroom, I promise not to believe all the stories I hear about what goes on in your house."

Believe it or not, I know a teacher who has not received a single parental complaint in 30 years of dynamic teaching.

Jim Cross is a true living legend in the town of Los Alamitos, California. After graduating from Stanford, where he played football on the same team with Jim Plunkett, he officially entered his chosen profession in 1970.

Students learned immediately that in "his" class, they not only had a very knowledgeable instructor, but also a guide and a friend who truly cared about them.

What made him stand out among most history teachers is that he also taught about the future.

Jim and his good friend, Jay Green, developed what they called the "Utopia Project." The students were given four weeks to develop their idea of a perfect society. They had to create their own governmental, educational, judicial and economic systems. They were urged to live out the cultural traditions they would encourage.

It was one of the most successful projects I have ever seen created in a classroom. The sub-text to the lesson was that everyone had the power (if they would choose to use it) to create the future they wanted to live.

He expanded on the idea when he left Junior High School to enter the world of sophomores, juniors and seniors. He added a new class to the curriculum, "Future Studies," which involved the basis of the "Utopia Project" he and his friend Jay had worked on. It was an elective, and had a waiting list of students eager to sit in on this master teacher's presence.

Now we come to Jim's special secret. The first three weeks of every semester, he would call the parents of each one of his students and say something similar to this:

"Hi, Mr. and Mrs. Smith, I'm Jim Cross, and I have the privilege of being your child's teacher for world history. I just wanted to call and introduce myself and tell you how much his/her success means to me. If ever you have any questions or if there is any problem I should know about, please feel free to call the school, and I promise to get back to you that very same day. You have a standing invitation to visit my class any time you desire. I'm sure that in working together, we can create a happy and productive year."

You can imagine the response. Most parents had never experienced such effort and consideration from a teacher since the early elementary years. In their eyes, Jim Cross could do no wrong.

There is no honor a teacher can be awarded that has not come Jim's way. Along with making every one of his students completely knowledgeable about his subject, he had also filled their hearts with great memories.

Jim utilized pillars of civility. Other notable teachers have used the same pillars, such as Marjorie Blevins Boor, who is a former student of mine and now teaches English, Linda Sackett, who is a sixth grade teacher, and by so many thousands of other instructors in our children's lives

Every one of their students is treated with courtesy and kindness. They know they are appreciated, and every lesson is based on the integrity of the instructor. In the way the lessons are so carefully constructed, they experience a daily example of commitment. They don't see themselves as having to work for their teachers, but as developers of creativity in patient cooperation.

They know their teachers have the courage to teach with total integrity.

All problems, scholastic or personal, are met with compassion, and their progress is constantly watched and encouraged. Finally, they know that their teachers know what they don't know and have the humility to admit whenever they are wrong (which is seldom, but it does occasionally happen).

I wish every one of you could visit classrooms such as these. You would see true Celebrations of Civility.

TREASURED REFERRALS

"Hey, son, come here."

The somewhat shocked seventh grader approached the new Principal, Warren Bratcher.

"I saw what you just did."

"What did I do, sir?" asked the hesitant student.

"Without anyone telling you to, you picked up a piece of paper and put it in the trash barrel. I accuse you of taking pride in your school. Are you guilty or not?"

"Well, I do like seeing the campus clean, and Joe, the custodian, is my friend, so I just thought I'd help him out." The boy replied with the frightened look beginning to be replaced with a slight smile.

"Okay, then, we'll add friendship and loyalty to your other crimes. Come to my office after school," boomed the Principal.

Somewhat pleased but totally confused, the young boy wandered off to his class, wondering if he was going to go to another part of "The Twilight Zone" while on his way.

Warren looked over at me (I had been standing nearby watching this entire exchange) and smiled. "I'm dedicated to catching my students doing something right," he said. "Nothing positive escapes me."

Later, he showed me the letter he wrote for the boy to take home to his parents. It went something like this:

Dear Mr. and Mrs. Jones,

Today, your son spent part of his time picking up trash that was not his. He did it for no reason other than that he is a very cooperative young man who takes pride in his school.

It is my feeling that you have something to do with this unusual behavior, and I must warn you that students who exhibit your son's attitude are usually saddled with awards they have to carry home.

Thank you for living in our district.

Sincerely,

Warren Bratcher

If he spied someone helping a teacher after school or staying late to study in the library or voluntarily helping a custodian, the child was called into his office and given a similar letter.

Also, handwritten letters went home to those who participated in school activities. Going to the Principal's office was considered a treat—unlike any school I had ever seen. Students vied for his attention through positive action.

His example created one of the happiest campuses I have ever observed.

His watchful appreciation created a positive example that most of the staff eventually tried to emulate.

Another Principal I worked with named Chuck Darrington had a similar attitude. His goal was to make sure his teachers would receive every possible award, and, in turn, many of his teachers created awards to give to their students.

The word appreciation means to grow in value. Both Warren Bratcher and Chuck Darrington increased the value of their schools based on their insistence that what was done right deserved more attention than what was done wrong.

In olden days it was believed that might MADE right. Later, under the leadership of inspired leaders such as King Arthur, as portrayed in the musical *Camelot*, there was a change. Might was used FOR right. Today, under the leadership of people like Bratcher, Darrington, Jaimie Escalante, Marva Collins and so many others, RIGHT IS CREATING MIGHT in a very positive sense.

Too often we underestimate the *power*

of a touch, a smile, a kind word, a listening ear,

an honest compliment or the smallest act of caring,

all of which have the potential to turn a *life* around.

— Leo F. Buscaglia

As you read earlier, my mother taught me to make sure to meet and appreciate at least one new person a day. What follows is how taking her advice led to the creation of one of the great friendships of my life.

THE OPPORTUNITY OF FRIENDSHIP

Have you ever watched people walk? Most folks do just that—they walk. But there are a very small percentage of people who *walk someplace*. Even if they are in the middle of a group of "walkers," they stand out. They emanate positive energy as they move with a confident sense of direction.

For years now, I never pass up the opportunity to meet one of these "energy emanaters." It all started the day that I met a young man named Mark Till. Just by the way he carried himself, you could tell that he was going for goals and dreaming dreams.

Speaking of Dreams, one of my big dreams was to produce Rogers and Hammerstein's *Carousel* at the junior high level. I had a great cast with one exception. I didn't have a male lead to play the difficult role of Billy Bigelow.

I was standing by my classroom one day when I saw him walking toward the gym. I called out, "Hey! Hey Mark Till! Come here a moment, please." He quickly changed direction and, with a confused look, approached me. Now, understand, I had never met him, but there was something in his bearing that made me feel I could trust him. So I did something I had never done before or since. I cast someone in a play without ever seeing him act.

"You want to be in a play?" I asked.

He thought for a moment. "Sure, why not." he said.

"Good," I replied. "It's the lead in a musical called *Carousel*."

"A what?" he stammered. "I've never sung a note in my life!"

"I don't care," I said. "I have a feeling you can do anything."

And he did! *Carousel* was one of the five most successful shows out of the 200 I directed during my career as a drama teacher.

That was only the beginning. He started out as my student, and like so many others before and after him, he became my friend. Eventually, he became my brother, as well.

He returned after graduation to help me produce more plays. He helped to plan and supervise our Academy Award Banquets. He reached some students I felt too old to understand. He was there on Dad's final evening before he passed away.

One show he really helped on after graduating was *Up The Down Staircase*. The girl who was playing the lead, Danelle Bensted, was one of the all time greats to ever grace my classroom. Now, Mark was in college by this time, and a lot of the ninth grade girls developed crushes on him. But not Danelle. Her dad was a football coach, and Mark enjoyed his company. He spent many evenings watching sports on TV with him. Meanwhile Danelle didn't pay much attention to Mark at all.

Mark was having a great social life in college, dating a large number of beautiful young ladies. But he kept saying things like "You know, Jack, I have a lot more fun with that kid Danelle than I do with these women."

Several years later, there was a knock at my door at two in the morning. There stood Mark. "Jack...," he moaned, "Danelle's not a kid anymore."

A few months later, I had the privilege of speaking at their wedding.

They have both excelled in education and youth ministry, and have blessed the world with two of the most dynamic young boys you'll ever see, Robbie and KC Till, two of my adopted nephews.

I hope this story encourages you to "call out" to people you wish to know. Look at all the blessings I would have missed if I had let shyness speak to me and silence my tongue.

Second and most important, I wanted you to meet Mark, for in a very simple, quiet way, he has helped to change the world.

For students to succeed, they must be willing to learn from their teachers. However, as a society, we must be dedicated to giving them teachers that will show them the stars and not the mud. As you well know, much of our popular culture teaches self-destructive behavior. This is the story of one such victim.

UNWISELY GIVEN

This was not the first time I saw her crying as she sat off by herself. In today's world where the media is constantly lying to young people about many things, no lie creates as much misery as the lie being told about sex.

For centuries, society taught us that a sexual union was to symbolize commitment and was reserved for marriage. Granted, many people have fallen short of that goal, but the ideal created positive caution and often caused young people to put off taking that "one big step" until it was right.

Studies have shown that the younger a person is when they have their first sexual encounter, the more certain it is that sex will control their lives and not be the wonderful experience that they will choose to add to life later on.

The young lady of whom I spoke in the beginning of the story had been deceived into thinking that sex was love, and she, being human and wanting love, had freely given her sexual favors to any boy who desired them. This had led to the most insulting name-calling anyone had ever experienced. She had been used and abused by a very large number of boys who had heard how willing she was. After having their "fun," they would then act like they didn't even know her.

I asked her why she had let so many boys take advantage of her.

"They're my friends," came the reply, "and I don't want to hurt their feelings."

"They're your friends?" I questioned. "What if one of your girlfriends came by and suggested going to the mall, and you agreed? Now suppose you walked into a fashion shop and there was a sweater she liked. So she reached into *your* purse and took *your* money and bought it and then suggested you go to lunch. After lunch, she then reached into your purse again for your money. At that point you'd grab her hand and say, 'Stop! You've got my money.'

"What if she replied, 'So? I like your money. I love to touch your money. I love to feel your money. Your money gets me excited.

Your money makes me happy. So, if you don't let me use your money the way I want to use your money, we're not friends.' Would you keep someone like that in your life?" I asked.

"No, of course not," came the reply.

"What's the difference between that girlfriend and some boy who says, 'I love your body? I love to touch your body. I love to feel your body. Your body gets me excited. Your body makes me happy. If you don't let me use your body the way I want to, we'll never date again.'

"You see, just like your money, your body is only a temporary possession. You want someone to love you for who you are, not for what you have."

I am happy to report to you that she caught onto the concept immediately and understood it. I saw her three years ago in a grocery store and met her loving husband and enjoyed her two children.

Today, thanks to the self-deprecating messages issued by movies and television shows that portray sex as being the natural outcome of teenage dating, kids are treating each other as if they don't really matter.

Maybe the 1950s were repressed, and certainly they were filled with racial injustice, but people of all races were taught that there should be meeting, liking, caring, sharing, loving, commitment, marriage and *then* sex.

What has our so-called sexual liberation produced? More children are being born to unwed mothers, as well as increased sexually transmitted diseases, more stressed-out and unhappy relationships based on sex, and higher divorce rates. And some popular music lyrics now glorify treating women as sexual objects.

In treating the most intimate of all human interactions with a shallow callousness, we have more unhappiness than ever before despite the fact that our society has given us more items of leisure and convenience than any group of people have ever enjoyed throughout history. The average citizen of America has more convenience, eats better, and enjoys greater ease than the Pharaohs of Egypt, the Caesars of Rome, or the old Kings of Europe.

My parents met when they were nine, had their first kiss when they were 17, and their love lasted into their 80s, when they still would hold hands and occasionally neck when they thought no one was watching. Dad loved Mom so much that he fought off cancer for 17 years because he wasn't going to die before her. We never talked about it, but I am sure they really enjoyed sex. After all, they had four children.

There is a big difference between people who love you and those who love themselves being with you.

The most civil thing we can do for our young people is to reintroduce them to Romance... and to the joys of pure affection.

Seek out that particular *mental attribute* which makes you feel most deeply and vitally *alive*, along with which comes the inner voice which says, "This is the *real* me," and when you have found that attitude, *follow it*.

— William James

I would like to introduce you to Jennifer Booth, a great student whose life was a great teacher.

GIVE FRIENDSHIP, GAIN A WORLD

One of the truly great programs on most high school campuses today is the foreign exchange program. American students and those from other countries exchange homes and schools for one year. Of the many problems that face this project, the greatest seems to be reluctance on the part of many American teenagers to step outside their social circle and meet new people... especially if those people have accents or different physical characteristics that are not considered "cool."

One of my very favorite students was a girl named Jennifer Booth. Jen was an explorer of personalities. She did not want to miss the opportunity to get to know anybody. She lived that old axiom, "A stranger is a friend I haven't met yet."

The idea of being exposed to new customs, traditions and ideas intrigued Jen. So she became one of the few American kids to join and take a very active part in the foreign exchange club. At one time or another, she had every member over to her house for dinner. Sometimes, they did the cooking and prepared favorite meals that were popular in their homeland. She taught them about America, and they shared their culture with her.

One day near graduation, she walked into a meeting where all of her new friends stood smiling, and with them stood her parents. Her Mom and Dad presented her with a round trip ticket to Europe. Her friends then gave her an itinerary of their homes where she would stay as their guest. She would spend a full summer in Europe at no expense except for transportation.

You can't out-give life. Jennifer had given them her time and friendship. In return her new friends had given her the world.

How does a child spell love? T-I-M-E. A way to spell friend is F-A-I-T-H. The great marriages must consist of T-I-M-E and F-A-I-T-H.

THE DANGER IN DOUBT
CAN PUT GOOD THINGS OUT

Sally's life was a miracle. For years, she had lived the well known expression, "Hell on Earth." Her husband, Greg, had been an alcoholic and been fired from job after job. To make matters worse, he had been arrested for Driving Under the Influence and had had his driver's license suspended long ago. Sally's paychecks had bailed him out of serious trouble more than once.

Then came the day... or should I say, came the awakening. Walking home from work one afternoon in a drunken stupor, he tripped and fell on top of his neighbor's little boy, who was playing on the front lawn. Sally heard the crying and rushed outside to discover that Greg's fall had broken the young lad's leg. Seeing the little boy in such pain, and for the very first time really seeing the hurt in his wife's eyes, Greg "woke up" to reality.

He finally saw that the alcohol, which he had considered his best friend, was truly his worst enemy.

The drunk that was Greg died that day, and in his place was a new Greg. Or perhaps I should say the Greg that Sally had really wanted to marry emerged.

His newfound dedication to Alcoholics Anonymous and his commitment to turning his life around amazed everyone in the neighborhood. He became such a good and trustworthy neighbor that the little boy whose leg he had broken started calling him Uncle Greg.

This new energy overflowed into his job, and the man who was close to being fired again rose to a position of top management.

There were new friends, creative activities and fantastic team-work. Sally had never believed she could be so happy.

Then, one night when Sally had prepared a special candlelight dinner to celebrate their anniversary, Greg was late coming home. When he finally arrived, he stumbled into the living room, knocked over the furniture, and fell on the floor, passed out.

"Oh Greg, how could you!" Sally screamed as she took her car keys and drove over to a friend's house to spend the night in tears.

The next morning when she drove home, she saw an ambulance in front of her house and two attendants were carrying out a body.

It was Greg.

"I hate alcohol!" Sally sobbed.

"What do you mean?" asked one of the paramedics. "He didn't have any alcohol in his system. He died of a heart attack. From what we can gather, he had been lying there quite a while, and was finally able to drag himself to a phone about two hours ago. It's a shame you weren't home. If we had been called earlier, we could have saved him."

If you love, you must trust. Trust rests on a foundation of Faith.

If you have ever been in
a real *tragic* or sad situation,
the *words* that come out are
hopelessly *inadequate*...

— Erika Slezak

I AM A LAWYER

I know you may be laughing, as there have been more jokes written and ridicule directed at my profession than any other, and much of it has been justified. But there are others of whom you may not have heard...

There are others of us who have put principle ahead of profit... those of us who have followed conscience instead of consensus.

There are those of us who have defended the defenseless... worked for the weak and promoted progress...

We who have fought for freedom of expression, even for those with whom we may disagree...

Because of us, wars are fought with words... Logic instead of lances... Argumentation instead of armies.

Black and white may be found on the printed page, but the color of the skin of the reader does not matter to us.

Rather than believe that 'Might makes Right' we choose to use 'Might *for* Right.'

We are the ones who fought to open doors of opportunity for women, minorities and individualists.

We have often sided with the poor against the privileged.

We have not considered 'who' might be right but rather 'what' is right.

Pharaohs, Emperors, Kings and Judges have made judgments depending on the tone of the times or popular opinion... But we are the seekers of justice who have worked to enshrine rule by LAW... which is no respecter of persons but only of principle.

Throughout the ages, philosophers, statesmen, humanitarians, people of faith and great thinkers have toiled and sacrificed to advance the cause of humanity... but it has been up to the lawyers to solidify those advancements and put a fortress of law around them to protect those advancements.

Perhaps more than any other professionals, I am totally aware of the imperfections to be found in members of the human race, which is why I champion the freedoms of speech, thought, religion and the press... the more people 'think' and think out loud, the greater the odds that out of the confusion of ideas may emerge the certainty of truth...

We have reversed foolish decisions made by many of our predecessors...

We have not pursued popularity but have been devoted to principle...

We have championed the Constitution; we have fought for freedom. Because of lawyers, conflicts have been resolved in courtrooms not cemeteries...

We often live and labor in the sanctuary of silence, as we have dueled with doubt...

You will not often read about us and what we have accomplished ... but walk with me down any street in any town, and you will see the evidence of our dedication in a more 'just' and 'lasting' society.

To me, a lawyer is basically the person that

knows the rules of the country.

We're all throwing the dice, playing the game,

moving our pieces around the board,

but if there is a problem, the lawyer is

the *only person* who has read the

inside of the top of the box.

— Jerry Seinfeld

TOUCHED BY A GENERATION

About the time the first radio entertained across the nation, and the automobile was becoming more and more the transportation of choice, and the telephone was eliminating distance ... YOU arrived.

Your childhood and the Great Depression occurred in the same decade, and despite hard times, you created new professions.

Then came the most heinous war in history. Destructive forces entered the World by way of the Third Reich and Japanese Imperialism, and you fought to create peace.

You navigated our course to successfully meet and overcome the challenge of Communism.

Then came Bigotry and Prejudice. You helped to start the march toward making equality a reality.

There were diseases. You came forth with new medicines.

There was poverty. Your humanity revived hope.

Under your capable leadership, Congress and other institutions throughout the land started to move away from being just one color and one gender and began to reflect more and more the real America.

Your energy entertained us with movies, plays, paintings and productions that captured our interest, tickled our funny bones, healed our hearts and stimulated our spirits.

You reached into the souls of your imagination and planted seeds of beauty, melody and inspiration, so that galleries, theaters and concert halls became uplifting cathedrals of culture.

You built bridges that united us and buildings that reached for the stars.

Throughout your life, while still being very human and capable of mistakes and poor judgment, more often than not, you met:

Confusion with Compassion,
Hatred with Humor,
Evil with Empathy,
Worry with Wisdom,
Fear with Faith,
Despair with Dedication,
Hopelessness with Humanity,
And especially...
    you fought cruelty using an implement called Civility.

The Egyptians had their Pharaohs. The Greeks had their Gods. The Romans had their Caesars. And they all failed and fell.

But we had You ...

From all walks of life, from every country around the world, you joined together to promote and proudly protect this dream called America.

And it still stands with all of its faults and shallow indulgences and occasional mob hysteria. It still holds the torch of endless possibilities and eventual humanity among humans.

But you still have gifts to give. You put us on the moon. Now we need to learn from your wisdom in how to live among the stars.

You increased our ability to communicate, and now we need to reflect your intelligence to help us make sure that what we say is worthwhile.

There are times when we carry the seeds of appreciation around with us for so long that we almost lose our chance to share them with the ones we are most appreciative of...

It is courtesy moving past crudeness.
It is consideration replacing contempt.
It is cooperation out-performing conformity.
It is joy dissolving depression.
It is substance overcoming shallowness.
It is appreciation diffusing anger.
It is generosity eclipsing the 'get mine' attitude.
It is sincerity melting away sarcasm.
It is faith triumphing over fear.
It is hope that heals hopelessness.

Above all it is kindness keeping compassion's constant vigil.

It is, I believe, the *greatest generation*

any society has ever produced.

— Tom Brokaw

Mothers of sons deserve special medals. As often their patience and love are tested to unbelievable limits. Fathers don't have it that easy either.

ANNE FRANK WAS RIGHT

Whenever a family moves into a new neighborhood, it usually takes time to get acquainted. However, because of my two brothers, the Schlatters became an integral part of a small town near St. Louis, Missouri, inside of one week.

George was six and Al was three at the time that we moved to this small town. They both had a sweet tooth, and on the day that the moving van arrived at the new house, they requested some money for candy as Mom and Dad were unpacking the newly arrived boxes. "I'm sorry, boys, I don't have any money with me right now," Mom told them.

Taking this to mean the family was broke, my ingenious brothers hit on a plan to save the Schlatters from starvation. Putting on their oldest clothes and pulling their wagon, they went up one side of the street, knocked on every door and said something like this. "Good day. We're da Schlatter boys, and our Mamma and Daddy don't have any money for food. We were hoping you have some old stuff you don't need that we could sell and buy Mom and Dad dinner tonight."

Needless to say, there was not one heart that was not truly touched by this tragic tale of poverty.

After getting their wagon full of old lamps, mittens, toys, and other discarded objects, they went down the "other" side of the street, gave the same speech and sold everything.

The next two days saw a parade of neighbors coming over to the house with hams, vegetables, baked bread and desserts.

Naturally, all these good Samaritans were shocked to see a healthy mother and father who were surrounded by very good furniture. They were also saddened to hear about two little salesmen who were sick to their stomachs (a lot of candy can do that).

But the laughter carried on for weeks. George and Al became the legends of the neighborhood, and Mom and Dad were blessed with new friendships, some that would last the rest of their lives.

You might say it was a rare miracle brought about by the innocent faith of two little boys that touched the kindness that dwelt so deeply in the hearts of their neighbors.

Years after this incident, Anne Frank, a little Jewish girl hiding from Nazi oppression, expressed in a single sentence the essence of what might explain the whole experience...

"People are really good at heart."

Bread for *myself* is a material question.
Bread for my *neighbor* is a spiritual one.

— Nikolai Berdyaev

People just want to know where they can find love, greatness and opportunity. This well-known little parable, which has appeared in just about every culture, religion and philosophy since the beginning of recorded time, might serve as a spiritual compass.

THE HIDDEN HOPE

It seems that after the task of creation had been completed, there remained one small task to be accomplished.

God called the angels together for a conference. "As you all know, the last gift we wish to bestow on humanity is its 'supreme greatness,' the power that will give people total control over all circumstances, problems and situations. But if we just hand them the power outright, they will take it for granted and not give it the respect and honor it deserves. So we must hide it, but the question is where?"

The angel of the sea suggested that it be put on the bottom of the ocean. The angel in charge of the earth suggested it be hidden in the remotest jungle. The angel of the mountains felt that the highest peak on the earth would be perfect. The angel of the heavens put forth the idea that placing it in on the farthest star would be most formidable.

Then stepped forth the timeless one, who, using his great vision that saw past, present and future, pointed out that someday humanity will come forth with ships called submarines to explore the ocean's very depths; that no continent will be safe from the unending curiosity planted in their creation; that people's determination will drive them to attain every summit on earth, and their genius will one day carry them beyond the stars.

Then the most humble angel came forth with the perfect suggestion. "Why not put it in one place where busy humans will never think to look? Let's put it inside each and every person's 'soul'!"

The humble one was greeted with enthusiasm and applause. Finally, the angel of questing approached God and asked, "Oh Great One, what do you call the fantastic power that can overcome all the difficulties your children down on earth will face?"

The Great One smiled and in a very soft but commanding voice said, "Love."

There are many people I have never met whose lives have taught me that a courageous soul can turn a loss into a great gain.

THE MAN WHO LOST HIS HANDS AND DISCOVERED HIS LIFE

Did you know that in the long history of the Academy Awards, there is only one actor who has won two awards for the same role in the same movie?

The most inspirational story to ever come out of Hollywood is the story of Harold Russell, who woke up in a veteran's hospital to discover he had lost his hands in the service of his country.

What hopelessness he must have felt! How do you go through life without those two valuable extensions? People have experienced the depths of depression with problems less terrifying.

It seems he was a student of Ralph Waldo Emerson, and as he lay in that bed of despair, one of the most powerful thoughts ever presented by any philosopher came to his mind. *It isn't important what was lost; what does count is what's left.*

He was still in possession of his eyesight, hearing, legs, voice and his "spirit." He could take these gifts and still be of service. He went out of his way to encourage others who had experienced tragic losses, and in doing that, he discovered greatness within himself that he had been unaware of up to that point.

During this time, Daryl Zanuck, head of Twentieth Century Fox, was planning to do a movie about returning veterans, and he wanted one of the characters to be played by an actual veteran who had overcome a physical handicap.

Needless to say, Harold Russell and his indomitable optimism and courage were brought to his attention.

The next time you are in a video store, go to the "classics" section and check out the film, *The Best Years of Our Lives*. After experiencing the cinematic miracle, you will feel the power to be found in families. Above all, you will feel a surge of courage fill your soul as you watch the realistic and heart-warming performance of Harold Russell, who took a hard blow from fate and used the experience to create one of the BEST LIVES EVER LIVED!

I AM A PROTECTOR OF PEACE
TRIBUTE TO THE MILITARY

I am proudly in the Military to be a Protector of Peace throughout the World. It is ironic that, in the act of fighting a war for human rights, my clear intention is for peace. I belong to a band of brothers and sisters who put the love of their country and its great traditions ahead of personal interest. To the members of my profession, nothing is so important as the lives and well being of my comrades, my family, my country ... and of all humanity.

We carry heavy loads... the memories, hopes and loves of those we have left behind. It is not for a flag that we fight but for what the flag represents... a nation of people! We have dreams of building a freer and more humane world, as we are motivated by love for those who are yet to come. The memories of the sacrifices made will walk and talk in the hearts of those we leave behind.

It is my mission to be a Peace Keeper... armed with weaponry that has the potential to put an end to any inhumane and heinous act. I am also armed with candy, toys, smiles and compassion. It is my mission to reach out daily to build bridges between people, ideas and lands. My primary goal is to bring the most important and basic fundamentals in life to the people whose country I have come to protect. I am here to provide security and to peace between people, and to cooperatively develop plans for building a greater humanity...

Because of us, it is possible to bring in supplies for the war-torn, and gleams of light become more visible.

Yes, faith is still alive because of us, the soldiers, sailors, flyers, officers, administrators, chaplains, doctors and nurses. I am deeply humbled by the magnitude of what I am here to do. We are on a life's mission to be the Heroes of Hope... the proud proclaimers of potential, the messengers of meaning, the legionaries of love...

For centuries, winning the war against any inhumanity has been the goal of every army... and yet, our victories are not complete until we have created something better to take the place of that which was once destructive and inhumane...

We fight the good fight so that people will have the freedom to discuss and joust with ideas... where all opinions are considered and the destiny of children is never out of sight...

And so we stand on the horizon of a new day... Our weapons laid down and our hands clasped in a prayer... to make a reality of the Dream of PEACE ON EARTH, GOODWILL TO ALL ... Amen

THE MILITARY FAMILY

I remember the day 'he' was born... the baby who grew into our treasured Son. The first time I held 'her' in my arms, I thought "Thank you, God, for this precious present, our princess, our Daughter."

'He' was my protector, my role model, my teacher, my Brother. Thanks to 'her' I understood girls; she was my playmate, my friend, my Sister.

When 'he' walked into my life, loneliness left while joy and a true sense of purpose took its place... My Husband. Because of 'her' my heart grew wings of tenderness and love... My Wife.

Today, the son, the daughter, the brother, the sister, the husband, the wife, all are dedicating their lives to military service.

They put themselves in mortal danger in far-away places.

They carry broken bodies to be healed in military hospitals.

They fly their jets protecting their comrades on the ground.

They serve on ships in waters far from our home.

They train new recruits on obstacle courses, in gymnasiums and classrooms, or work in their offices supporting and preparing to lead their troops while strengthening the doubters and the broken hearted.

We miss their affection, guidance, sense of fun and sharing... but we live in the wisdom and wonder of their teachings and unswerving love and dedication.

For we are also Warriors who fight our battles in silence and with letters, memories and prayers.

We are the families of those who serve our country in the military... while our bodies are here at home, our hearts live with them on military bases and in foreign lands.

We have inspired their sense of mission; we are the reason they serve. Our pictures and love letters are carried into conflict and looked upon with affection during the 'silent' times...

We are the sustainers of Humanity who give the most important part of our lives to make a better world...

We are the families who spend our lives in support and love for them as they serve, and we take comfort from the knowledge that we also serve in our quiet but dedicated ways...

We know that because of the sacrifices and dedication of our loved ones, hope, freedom and charity live...

We know that 'Our' families are helping the world become more aware of the Family of Humanity...

Former student Mindy Dow has had tremendous success producing some of the biggest events in the American culture. But she is more than a producer; she is also a wonderful teacher, as you will see in the following story.

THE WINNING AUDITION

"Show people" are among the most courageous souls on the earth. Naturally, it can hurt a salesperson if, after a presentation, their product is rejected. But an actor, actress, singer or dancer who has had an unsuccessful audition feels like they themselves have been rejected, and they have to rebuild that broken self-esteem and get to another tryout, knowing full well that they may suffer the same negative result.

I have seen more than my share of tears and sad faces from the un-cast, which is why I want you to meet one of the most fantastic personalities to ever grace the stage of my life.

Her name is Mindy Dow. She was always a performer. She was so good that when she was accepted in the World Famous Young Americans, she set a record as the youngest member ever admitted up to that time.

But, in her heart of hearts, she was always a producer and a director. Her record of success is astonishing. She has organized performances for such organizations as Disneyland, Coca-Cola®, and the Super Bowl and produced shows in Japan and on American Aircraft Carriers.

I don't think there are many big stars she hasn't met or worked with. I know for sure there's no friend she has ever forgotten.

She has turned every neighborhood where she has lived into a family. One year, she was given the fantastic position of organizing the "Fan Fest" for the Major League All-Star Game in San Diego. The position was important, filled with status and responsibility, not to mention great pay. But she had it written into her contract that she would not be working the fourth of July because she had organized a fireworks party for her friends and wouldn't ever let them down.

That's Mindy. For 27 years, I have seen her always put people first.

Now back to the subject of auditions. Whenever a performer tried out for a show Mindy was directing, they walked out of the audition with a smile, whether they were rejected or accepted. Once I was privileged to sit through six hours of outstanding performances in an audition that could only accept one out of 10 of the hopefuls.

Mindy conveyed to every single person that they had done her a big favor by donating their time to audition, and she never failed to discover and comment on some outstanding quality of their talent she had discovered during their audition.

Such compassion has been returned to her time and time again. One beautiful day in March 1999, I had the honor of speaking at her wedding. She joined her life with a fantastic young man, James Broodly. I have spoken for and/or attended over 120 weddings, and this one was the most unique. The guests flew in from Europe and from 10 different states. Because of her deep commitment to friendship and all the qualities that make up Civility, the loyalty of her friends knew no limits. There is a great play called *A Man for All Seasons*. Maybe someday a play will be written about Mindy. It should be called *A Friend for all Situations*.

Ask "WHAT CAN I GIVE?"...

And *Life* replies "WHAT CAN I GIVE TO YOU?"

— John Wayne "Jack" Schlatter

I love showing off my students to my readers. Meet Jill McIntyre.

KEEPING THE FAITH CAN BE YOUR FORTUNE

Jill was every teacher's dream. For over two and a half years, Jill had been an outstanding student. It would usually take 100 points to get an "A" in my class, and Jill would usually score 150 points each semester. Whenever she was cast in a play, she would show up at the first rehearsal with her lines already memorized. She never gossiped and always had an encouraging word for her fellow students.

As her final year drew to a close, we had one play left on the agenda. Jill's class was loaded with female talent. In honor of all they had accomplished together, I had chosen the play *Stage Door*. It had 20 great parts for women. Jill had just played one of the leads in *To Kill a Mockingbird*. For *Stage Door* she wanted to play the comedy part of Bobbie, who was very funny but only had about 20 lines.

Now put yourself in Jill's shoes for a moment. For two and a half years, you have poured your heart and soul into this drama department. Day in and day out, you have heard your teacher quote Napoleon Hill, "If you can conceive it and believe it, you can achieve it." It was a code you had lived by. So you show up to hear the cast announced with your usual excitement.

The cast is announced, and you not only don't get the part you wanted, you get *no part*! The backstage and production staff is announced and you are not included.

It's the final show of the year, and you have absolutely nothing to do with it despite the fact that your record of accomplishment is greater than any of those who were cast. Is there a chance you might be a little bit upset with your instructor?

Afterwards, I walked over to Jill, expecting an angry outburst or torrent of tears. Her eyes were moist, but there were no tears or anger. "I've always trusted you," she said. "I'm not going to quit now."

As the kids walked out, I was the one who had to fight tears. Her loyalty and faith astounded me. She would not let one negative occurrence undo years of friendship and mutual accomplishment. She was aware that I treasured her, and she chose to believe that whatever I did, I had my reasons.

And I did have my reasons, or REASON, and it was a big one. I had noticed a vacant spot on the calendar and had obtained a verbal approval from the front office to do one more play before *Stage Door*, but I couldn't announce it until I had received written approval.

You see, Jill wasn't going to have time to do any work on *Stage Door* because she was going to play the leading role of Anne Sullivan in *The Miracle Worker*.

Buckminster Fuller said he was a reverse paranoid in that he believed life was secretly plotting to do him good. Since knowing Jill and young people like her, I find it easy to share that philosophy. After all, the force that gave us such a great computer that we call a brain, those two magnificent cameras on either side of our nose we refer to as eyes, and a stereo set that requires no batteries, which have the label of ears, must have something wonderful for us in mind. Such a force that has given so much and more must have designed us for happiness and good fortune. Maybe the greatest blessing of all comes from life itself.

Faith is to believe what you do not see;
the reward of this faith is to *see* what you *believe*.

— Saint Augustine

As I have mentioned before, one of the great privileges I have enjoyed as a teacher is becoming an adopted member of many families. As you will see, it is a wonderful and educational experience.

THE TRUTH AND THE COURAGE

Marty Crowe's son and daughter couldn't be more my nephew and niece than if I myself had been born a Crowe.

We love to give to children, especially during holidays and birthdays. Also, giving advice is great fun, especially on those rare occasions when it is heeded. However, in our "giving" we should remember one of the most civil things we can do is to be willing to receive from them.

When the kids were very young, Matt and Jesyka started giving me some very important lessons.

At the time Matt was about nine years old, the Crowes and I lived in very close proximity. Now, Marty and his wife Laurie had established a definite family life together, and along with all the love and spontaneity, there had been definite routines. Breakfast was in the morning, dinner at night, church on Sunday and all possessions in their proper places. This was the life Matt had experienced, but he had never seen the life of a bachelor at close range, especially not one as quirky as his Uncle Jack (me).

During this time, I had been achieving a lot of success, and I am embarrassed to admit that I was starting to develop an exaggerated idea of my own importance.

In short, I was starting to become a little boorish until one night when Matt very gently became my teacher and put me in my place.

He and I were going to a video store, and I turned the car a little too sharply and hit a curb. Visions of a possible flat tire or a soon-needed wheel alignment flashed through my mind, and I said a couple of words that no adult should say in front of a child.

"I'm sorry, Matt," I said.

"That's okay," he replied. "I've heard those words before."

"Yea, but it's not a good example," I proclaimed.

It was then that this nine year-old child reached over and gently patting my arm, saying, "Uncle Jack, I love you and you're really a nice man, but being an example is just not your field."

The air went out of my over-inflated ego like a balloon that had been punctured by a pickaxe.

To understand the power of Jesyka's lesson, I must first relate an incident about a time when I walked into a restaurant and almost bumped into Wilt Chamberlain, former All-Star center for the Los Angeles Lakers. My head came up to his chest. I must admit I was quite intimidated despite his friendly manner.

Now, back to Jesyka. When she was about three and a half, she received a shot from a hypodermic needle to help her get over an illness. As was and still is her style, she informed the entire world that she did not like it!

One week later, Laurie took her back to the doctor for a checkup. The doctor always came out of his office to greet the children before he took them into his room (or, as Jesyka called it, his "dungeon").

"Hello Jesyka," he said with a big smile.

At this point, my three and a half-year-old niece who was a little over two feet tall, held out her hand like a traffic cop.

"Stop right there!" she commanded. "What are you going to do to me?"

"Why, nothing Jesyka, I just want to make sure you're alright."

"I'M FINE, PERFECTLY FINE," said the little general, "AND I DON'T NEED TO GO IN THERE!"

Now, think about this for a moment. I was intimidated by a man who was one and a half times my size, and to Jesyka that doctor must have appeared to be the size of Wilt Chamberlain. But that did not stop her courageous outburst.

Matt went on to receive a full scholarship at Cornell University, after a high school career where he achieved a straight "A" average and was an All State guard on a championship team. He is still gently sharing the truth when it is needed.

Jesyka became a fantastic artist, horseback rider and entertainer, and she is still taking strong stands for what she believes.

Yes, they are my nephew and niece, but in so many more ways, they are still my teachers.

My brother Bob and his fantastic wife Mickey have been great teachers. And their four best students are their daughters.

UNITED THEY SOAR

I wish you could meet my four nieces who are the daughters of my brother Bob and his wonderful wife Mickey. They are all very accomplished in their own professional fields of endeavor.

The oldest is Debbie, the most loving person I have ever known and the greatest teacher I have ever seen.

Pam is tremendously brilliant and is one of the most successful and respected school Principals in all of California.

Kim has taken a strong sense of independence and used it to create a very successful career in business.

Then there is Jamie, whose dedicated sense of compassion has saved countless lives.

They are all devoted wives and mothers. You might say they are almost too good to be true, but I'm prejudiced.

As marvelous as their independent successes have been, what they have accomplished together is what has earned them royal thrones in my own personal hall of fame.

For over 40 years, they have remained totally united and supportive of each other. When one of them faced a crisis, the other three have dropped everything to be there to help and to comfort. Their nieces and nephews are loved by each one of their aunts with a complete devotion.

Since Bob has left the earth to join others from my family, Mickey has been like a fifth sister to her daughters. All gatherings are filled with fun and laughter. What has always amazed me is that when they all come together at one time, they are so excited to be in each other's presence that they all talk at once. What is totally astounding is that they all understand what is being said.

I have seen many siblings keep a bond all of their lives, but for the most part, there is a drifting apart after the age of 30.

Once I was talking with Jamie, and I asked her how they had achieved this remarkable unity.

She smiled and told me the story.

"Well, Uncle Jack, when I was about five or six, my sisters and I had been in one argument after another. My Dad took us outside and gave each one of us a stick and asked us if we would break them. It was simple to do as he asked. Then, he took four more sticks, which were the same size as the other ones, and bound them together and asked us to break the pack. Try as we could, we were unable to do it. Dad smiled and told us that we were looking at our future. We could stand apart and be easily broken, or we could unify and remain indestructible. None of us ever forgot that day.

Since that time, they have experienced the loss of all four of their grandparents, their father, two uncles and one aunt. They have had many triumphs to be sure, but there have been illnesses, business failures, heartaches and lots of disappointments; but tied together with the strings of loyalty, appreciation and humor, the bundle of love remains unbroken.

To the outside world we all grow old.

But not to *brothers* and *sisters*.

We know each other as we always were.

We know each other's hearts.

We share private family jokes.

We remember family feuds and secrets,

family griefs and joys.

We live outside the touch of time.

— Clara Ortega

I have told you of Dr. Jim Young, whose reach goes beyond eternity, as you will see in the following story.

THE GREAT GRANDFATHER OF PEPPERDINE

My favorite college instructor of all time was Dr. Jim Young. He was the head of the drama department at Pepperdine College. Along with teaching me how to perform, he had a life-long impact on me and eventually on every student who would walk into my classroom.

We did many productions, such as *Midsummer's Night Dream*, *Carousel*, *Lost Horizon* and *Androcles and the Lion*. And every year we would do Thornton Wilder's immortal classic, *Our Town*. It was one of the most cherished traditions in Pepperdine's history.

Every show started off with young actors and actresses coming together as a cast. By the time the final curtain on the final performance came down, we had become a family.

Dr. Jim Young had many methods of bringing this miracle about, but the most important one was the meeting we would have before each show. People shared what the play had taught them and what they had learned from each other.

The basic message of *Our Town* was to love life while you live it; every, every second was never lost on any of us.

Years later, I stood before my first cast of *Our Town* at Izaak Walton Middle School where I was teaching. I felt Dr. Young's presence. It seemed like I heard his voice say, "Teach them to love, to love the play and especially to love each other."

Throughout my 30 years in the teaching profession, I continued to produce that play every three years. Veterans of *Our Town* have made up quite a fraternity. In 1976, former students from 10 different productions dating back to 1959 attended that year's performance. People who were years apart and had never met before acted like old friends because of their common love of *Our Town* and their sharing of mutual memories.

In 1982, I walked into Kennedy High School, not as a director but as a member of the audience to see *Our Town*, produced and directed by a former student of mine, Mark Till. I was invited to their pre-show meeting. "Hey Jim," I said to myself, "you have a grandson."

Mark later went to teach at St. Margurette High School, and his drama department was so big he hired one of his former students, Jeff Nowlin. Later, Mark moved on, and Jeff became head of the drama department. What was one of Jeff's first shows? You guessed it. *Our Town*. Mark and I attended the pre-show meeting together, and in a very special way, I felt the presence of Great-Grandfather Jim.

What an impact, what an influence that wise humble, kind, committed, appreciative gentleman has had on so many lives.

What was the secret for such success?

He found something he could love. In this case, it was a play and the message it presented.

He was committed and lovingly appreciative of everyone who took part in that project.

He taught subjects, but more important, he taught students.

He is still alive today, and in a very special way he will never die. His spirit and traditions continue to live in his students and his student's students.

I have been given the honor of speaking at the weddings of 22 former students, and I end each speech with that priceless quotation, "Love life while you live it, every, every second." And wherever he is, I know Great-Grandfather Jim is smiling.

I *teach*, I touch *eternity*.

— Christa McAuliffe,
The teacher who we lost as
she reached for the stars.

I AM A SPEAKER AND LEADER

I am a Speaker and Leader... I have traveled through time on waves of words empowered by those who spoke before my time.

I have stood with head bowed in admiration as Pericles told the citizens of Athens the whole world was the graveyard for fallen heroes.

I have walked the streets of Rome and heard Cicero proclaim that a good Speaker was a good Man speaking.

My self confidence became reinforced when first lady Eleanor Roosevelt told young people that no one could make them feel inferior without their consent...

I was in Washington D.C. when President Kennedy challenged his countrymen to ask not what their country could do for them but what they could do for their country... and years later, I was there when Dr. Martin Luther King woke up a sleeping nation with his Dream for a more just and humane society...

Hills of Hope grew in my soul at Gettysburg when President Lincoln pledged that this government of the people, by the people and for the people would not perish from the earth...

Courage was created in my soul when Franklin Roosevelt told us we had nothing to fear but fear itself, and when Ronald Reagan reminded us America was destined to be a shining city upon a hill...

I was inspired when Helen Keller spoke from her dark and silent world and told us that life was either a daring adventure or it was nothing...

John Kennedy best described the duty of a speaker in his tribute to Sir Winston Churchill when he said, "In England's darkest hour, and deepest peril... Churchill empowered the English language and sent it into battle..."

Churchill created courage in his countrymen when he challenged them to so conduct themselves that, if the British Empire and its Commonwealth lasted for a thousand years, men would say, "This was their Finest Hour."

While I am a speaker and leader, I must never forget my role as a dedicated listener... and as one who pays attention to the needs and desires of his audiences, for they are the true givers, as they have shared their time and attention with me.

As a speaker, I enjoy a unity with my audiences... whether we agree or disagree, we are united for a moment as we join in our mutual quest for new answers to old questions.

When I face my audiences it is my desire to use my words and thoughts to...

lead compassionately;
ignite inspiration;
forge faith in family;
find hope through humor;
explore the greatness in gratitude;
and to enrich the human soul with Energy.

I am a Speaker and Leader ...and it is my sincere prayer that the thoughts I utter, the memories I share, the laughter I love and the appreciation I generate will last forever...

You are not here merely to make a living.

You are here in order to enable the world to live more amply, with *greater vision*, with a finer spirit of hope and achievement. You are here to *enrich the world* and to impoverish yourself if you forget the errand.

— Woodrow Wilson

Life is a circle and we must remember that it is impossible to give without receiving even more.

AN ATTITUDE OF GRATITUDE CAN INCREASE LIFE'S ALTITUDE

As we get older, we get huge attacks of the "should-haves."

When I was growing up, my parents, brothers and other relatives made sure that I received many presents at Christmas and on my birthday. I remember calling my friends and telling them what I "got." I also remember that I seldom took the time to say "Thank You." I wish someone had pointed out that the gifts I received were the result of other people's sacrifices and giving. So it is that every happy memory of the past is tainted with a twinge of regret.

On the other hand, one of my greatest Christmas memories is the Christmas evening I stayed up all night after the family had gone to bed and cleaned up the whole house of all the holiday debris. The next morning everyone received the gift of a clean house, a work free day, and I was given a wonderful sense of self-satisfaction and the beautiful feeling that I had made a positive difference.

In giving our gifts, we should also give the receivers instruction in the art of appreciation.

The truth of this concept was driven home to me on the closing night of one of the most successful shows we had ever presented.

Before the last performance of every play, I had made it a tradition to give all the people involved letters telling them what they had meant to the show and thanking them.

On this particular occasion, I had been in a rush and I didn't take the time to write any letters, thinking it wouldn't matter much.

After our last cast meeting, I wished everyone well and opened the door for them to get in their assigned place. But the kids just sat there.

"Come on everybody," I said, "There's an audience waiting out there."

One of the girls said, "Mr. Schlatter, you forgot to pass out the letters."

"Oh, I'm sorry, guys, I just didn't get around to it."

Another girl with tears starting to form in her eyes said, "Don't you like us?"

"Like you? I love you all. You're one of the best groups I've ever worked with."

"But you didn't write us," said another student.

"I didn't think they were that important," I said. "Now come on, let's go," I ordered.

The following Monday, various students came into my room with scrapbooks in which they had stored letters from previous shows. I felt terrible. There was never another cast and crew that didn't receive letters.

Why hadn't I written them? I guess it was because nobody had ever told me how much these things had meant. They had taken them for granted just as I had taken for granted all the presents I received in my youth.

Tides come in, tides go out.

The Sun rises, the sun sets.

When Gifts are given,

gratitude must be expressed.

— John Wayne "Jack" Schlatter

Opportunity has a great sense of humor. It brings us great blessings disguised as hardships.

LOSE THE STRUGGLE, LOSE THE SUCCESS

He was a kind-hearted little boy who couldn't stand to see any living creature in pain.

One day when he was playing outside, he saw a butterfly struggling to break out of a cocoon. Having such a kind heart and next to no education about nature, the little boy ran inside and took out his mother's sewing scissors. Then he went back outside toward the struggling butterfly. Once there, he very gently and lovingly cut the rest of the shell of the cocoon so the butterfly could come right out without having to go through any more struggle.

He then went back inside and returned his mother's scissors to the sewing cabinet. When he returned, he was shocked to see the butterfly lying on the ground, dead, a cat playing with its lifeless form.

What the little boy didn't know was that the struggle to break free of the cocoon is what develops the muscles in the butterfly's wings so it can fly.

Parents and teachers who are willing to create intelligent challenges and spend the time to tell the truth with kindness and compassion create healthy, productive children.

We must let our children know when and where the pilgrims landed, *and* we need to tell them *why* they came.

We teach what the Declaration of Independence says and what the Constitution says, *and* what they each *mean*.

We *love* them, *and* we allow the opportunities that will show them how to fulfill the obligation to loving *others*.

We make sure they know how to *exist*, and we lovingly show them how to *live*.

We model the simple truth written by Tom Paine, "The greater the conflict, the more glorious the triumph."

Once again I return to the major theme of this book. If we want to be effective, we must be willing to learn from each other.

PLEASE LISTEN TO ME

My three brothers and their wives blessed my parents with six wonderful granddaughters and one outstanding grandson. The rest of their grandchildren, they chose! I speak of many of my former students such as Marty Crowe, Kathy Abbot, Laurie Klatscher, Bill Bevill, Mindy Dow and especially Marjie Blevins.

I first met Marjie in 1971 when she was a shy seventh grader in my drama class. That was the *last* year anyone associated the word "shy" with Marjie. She was growing into a musical magician as her skill with the piano grew beyond talent into the realm of "gifted." She was so great and dependable that in 1974, while still in the ninth grade, she became my entire orchestra and choral director for our production of *Fiddler on the Roof.* She was no longer my student, for she became my co-director for musical after musical, which were so outstanding they drew larger audiences than most of the surrounding high schools.

Our bond grew stronger through the years. She helped me get through the passing of my parents, and I was there for her when her beloved Aunt Susie died.

She returned to play at our drama banquets and after she began her own teaching career, I held seminars for every one of her classes since 1987. Her record in education was fantastic. By her third year, she had won teacher of the year honors.

Then there was the inspirational arrival of her daughter, Rachel, and my godson, Ben.

I will never forget Marjie Blevins' piano recital; I honestly felt that I had been transported to heaven. But it was on another afternoon that with one sentence she totally changed my life.

It was a day when she was in the 10th grade; she came over to my school to see me during my preparation period. "May I talk to you?" she asked.

"Of course," I replied. I was used to students coming to me with problems. I'm not saying I ever helped, but I can say with confidence that I gave the longest speeches filled with the most platitudes in the history of education.

So naturally after two or three sentences, I interrupted her and proceeded to pontificate on how she could best handle her problem.

Suddenly, she held up one hand, like a traffic cop and with a very sincere smile and a gentle but firm voice said, "MR. SCHLATTER, I ASKED IF I COULD *TALK* TO YOU, NOT *LISTEN* TO YOU."

What a shock! What a Gift!

She taught me two things in that moment. First, most people don't want to be lectured to, they want to be heard. Second, you can have all the love in the world, you can share countless experiences, but no relationship can exist without TRUTH.

She could have very courteously listened to me while "watching the clock." But she had too much respect for our friendship to tolerate one phony moment.

Many people are afraid to hear the truth and even more are frightened to tell it. Since that day, when Marjie became my teacher, I have tried to follow her example. I can tell you after 25 years of experimenting and observing, I have discovered that the truth, told with honesty, kindness and compassion, positively serves healthy communication. The longer you try to keep it buried, the more it seethes until it overflows with a lava of broken friendships, vanished trust and destroyed relationships.

But please note, when having to utter a difficult truth, do it "Marjie Style," gently, kindly and with love.

There have been many other instances when the student became the teacher in our relationship. But that one afternoon was the most important. From that point forward, students of mine she has never met enjoyed "talking" to a teacher who really listened, thanks to her courageous intervention.

And so now that you have met Marjie Blevins Boor, you can understand why I feel she has come the closest to being the daughter this ol' bachelor never had.

To me, parents are the greatest unsung heroes of the earth. Despite thousands of years of human history, no one has really developed a child-rearing system that works all the time. Children have endured much pain caused by parents who were too lenient and by parents who were too strict. I have heard students complain that their parents were nosey, and two weeks later, I have heard those same young people upset that their mom and dad didn't spend more time with them.

What is a human being to do? Well, I have never found the right system either, but I have discovered a technique that never fails. I listen.

Listen.

Do not have an opinion while you listen

because frankly, *your opinion*

doesn't hold much water outside of Your Universe.

Just listen.

Listen until their brain has been

twisted like a dripping towel

and what they have to say

is all over the floor.

— Hugh Elliott

TEACHABLE MOMENTS

Little Jesyka Crowe had just finished her corn flakes, but there was still some milk in the bowl. Her brother, Matthew, was sitting in front of the TV, and to Jesyka his hair looked much too dry. So she did what any sensible four-year-old would do in such a situation. She walked over to him, stood behind him, and poured the remaining milk on his head, which got all over his clothes and slightly stained the rug.

And so it was that I was privileged to observe one of the greatest displays of positive parenting I have ever witnessed.

The little girl's mother calmly said, "Jesyka explain to me *what was going on for you* that you poured your milk on your brother's head?" To which Jesyka innocently responded that it simply looked like it would be fun to do ending with, "...and it was, wasn't it mommy?"

Please note how her mother, Laurie Crowe, handled the situation. Notice that she asked, "What" and not "Why." This teaches children how to access any feelings that might be in play. Then you can teach them how to "use their words" when something is upsetting them instead of using behavior to "act it out."

Upon understanding Jesyka's four-year-old intentions, which were for fun and not a result of a problem between herself and her brother (because if that were the case there would need to be a different conversation,) she proceeded to teach what behaviors were acceptable and what ones were not acceptable regarding whether or not to do "fun" things because it seemed like a good idea at the time.

She "made the time" to calmly teach and explain the specific consequences that would happen should Jesyka ever think it would be fun to make her brother her "target for fun" in this way again. She made it a point to calmly refer to the behavior as Jesyka's "choice."

Then, she did something marvelous!

She asked Jesyka to repeat back to her what she understood about what had just been explained, including her understanding of what specific consequences would happen should she choose to do it again.

After that, she held her little girl's hand and walked her over to get the towels and mop to clean up her brother and the mess on the floor, together.

To review: She did not criticize the child. She sought to "understand" first what was going on in the mind of the child, so the child would learn how to identify and speak her feelings. Only then did she identify the behavior that would not, from this day forward, be acceptable anywhere, at any time.

She clearly stated what the specific consequences would be should her daughter choose to do it again.

She reassured the child that she was loved, and regardless of what choices she made, she would nonetheless be loved just as much as she was before the bovine baptism.

She did NOT shame her daughter by saying she was "disappointed in her behavior," because she was four and it was, after all, normal, age appropriate behavior. She DID discuss places where having fun WERE acceptable and safe.

Marty and Laurie Crowe have made their home the most loving, supportive, educational and fun place to be, so there is nowhere to sneak off to in order to add more excitement to their lives.

From what I have observed over the years, families who gave skill development as their form of discipline, with kindness to their enforcement of the rules, create healthy, happy and productive children. Their homes are schools, recreation areas and sanctuaries. The parents live their lives with their children. Everyone is made to feel not just welcome but needed and appreciated.

I was 25 when I realized that the greatest friends I would ever have were my mom and dad. I was granted 20 years to do everything I could to say, "Thank You," and I was pretty successful at expressing my gratitude. But nothing could erase the pain I felt as I remembered all those times I took them for granted.

Most parents want what's best for their children. Teaching the principle of gratitude by modeling it, is one of the greatest gifts that a parent can teach their children.

As gratitude is nourished, the desire to join the Celebration is awakened, and the child becomes aware of a whole new life and a great truth.

My brother, Bob Schlatter, was the greatest public school counselor I've ever met. (This truth does not get him off the hook for all the dirty tricks he played on me when we were growing up!) He was a master at using analogies to prove a point. The following is an excerpt from a story he wrote, titled Sliding through the Diploma Factory, *and it tells about one of his successful encounters with two troubled students.*

LUBRICATIONS HELPS

John loved to race his bike competitively. Every Saturday he could, he entered a race on his bike.

When John was referred to his counselor for disrupting class and talking back to the teacher, he was asked, "Why do you hurry home on Thursday and Friday before a race?"

"I shine my bike up and get it all clean," John responded.

"Is that all?" asked the counselor.

"No," said John. "I grease the wheels and the chain."

When asked why, John said, "It makes the bike ride smoother. It goes faster and pumps easier with grease on the wheels and chain."

Matt, as a senior, loved to work on cars. He wanted to be a mechanic when he graduated. Indeed, he had a part-time job in a garage after school every day.

Matt was referred to the counselor for being argumentative with his teacher. His counselor asked him, "Do you put oil in your car's engine?"

Matt looked at the counselor as though looking at an idiot. "Of course," he shot back contemptuously, "the oil cuts down on the friction. Without oil, the friction would make the motor too hot. The cylinders would swell. The motor would burn up...you've GOT to have oil!"

When John was asked if a little "grease" would make his history class run smoother, and when Matt was asked if a little "oil" would cut down on the friction in his class, both boys understood immediately.

Friction between a teacher and a pupil causes heat. The heat causes anger, loss of temper, loss of control and loss of any chance of understanding.

Matt became interested in attention-getting techniques. He found that he could pay better attention if he observed the teacher. What did he wear? What mannerisms did he repeat? What section of the class did the teacher watch? With which faces did the teacher make eye contact most often?

After a month, Matt realized that the teacher wore one pair of slacks for a week at a time. He would wear a brown pair for a week, then a gray pair for a week. One day, on a Monday, the teacher wore a pair of slacks Matt hadn't seen before.

"Hey, Mr. Scharfin, are those slacks new?" asked Matt on the way out of class. "They really look good on you."

The teacher wore the same slacks for two more days, and Matt said nothing, but he noticed that Mr. Scharfin caught his eye more often for those two days. Each time the teacher looked at Matt, Matt would cast a glance at the slacks. On Thursday, the teacher changed slacks, wearing a checkered pair. After class, Matt pointed at the pants and said, "Sharp threads, Mr. Scharfin."

This time, the teacher said, "Thank you, Matt."

For two weeks, Matt complimented the teacher on any change of his attire. After two weeks, Matt realized a strange phenomenon... Mr. Scharfin was wearing a different pair of slacks every day. In fact, his entire grooming habits began to improve. Moreover, Matt's face was one with which he made contact more often than before. Also, Mr. Scharfin started to put forth more easily in his teaching.

I wish to point out most definitely that all of his compliments were sincere. Matt had just placed a little more oil in the crankcase to the benefit of both the teacher and the student.

Nothing makes people so worthy of
compliments as receiving them.
One is more *delightful* for being *told* one is delightful

— just as one is angrier for being told one is angry.

— Katherine F. Gerould

I DREAMED A DREAM

I was in a classroom with one student... never had I sensed such sadness.

"What is wrong, my friend?" I asked.

"I am so depressed because I am so angry," he replied.

"Who are you mad at?" I inquired.

"MYSELF." He answered, "I have made so many mistakes and let so many people down, I can hardly bare it. I have squandered opportunities, broken promises and engaged in countless selfish acts."

"Oh come now, you can't be as bad all that!" I said.

"Oh, I have done some good and helped a few folks, but nowhere near as many as I could have, if I hadn't been so messed up," he answered.

Suddenly I awoke with a strong sense of worry and concern for this lad.

How could he walk into tomorrow carrying such heavy loads of guilt and regret? And then I started to wonder how many others were like him, fully aware of their faults but totally ignorant of their virtues. What could I say or do to help such people?

Then the thought hit me. He didn't need a pep talk or an inspirational message, what he needed was a FUNERAL, and I would write the obituary.

And so I wrote...

Here he lies, buried under the mud and debris of broken dreams, frustrations, disappointments and the memories of countless mistakes that in some cases hurt or let others down.

On top of this grave are huge boulders of guilt.

Do not look for his body, it is not here, for he needs it to carry him into a new life, accompanied by friends who go by the names of appreciation, joy and love...

He will be missed by some, for he did try to make the world a better place.

But he had been fooled by the illusion that his enemies were exterior ones, who went by the names of "other people."

Believing this illusion gave free rein to those deadly interior ones such as fear, worry, self doubt, anger and immaturity.

They had been the creators of the misery.

However, for the most part, they have perished from the disease known as neglect, because our hero now has no time for them.

He walks into a new world a new creature, ready to encounter unmet friends, second and third and even hundreds of chances if they are needed, and to reacquaint with newly appreciated old friends.

The dreams once buried have been resurrected and live once again with a new energy.

In this new life, there is nothing to forgive or for which to be forgiven.

For any lasting effects of past mistakes can be corrected.

Now there is much to bless and for which to be blessed!

So it is that the gods of opportunity now roused from a long sleep have opened their doors anew and spread out their welcome mats.

A new day of inspiration is dawning on a life reborn, a life that will never die...

A few nights later I re-visited that Dream and that Classroom, and there "he" was, as if waiting for me.

"Thank You," he said. "Since that funeral, I have taken up a new profession, architecture. I am building a new creature with eyes of encouragement, a face filled with faith and a head that sends forth humor.

"You know every once in a while, I think of that fellow we buried because it seems like his ghost occasionally knocks on the door of my mind seeking entrance. I politely refuse him, for he taught me much, but I have no time for him... Now I truly understand what was meant by the saying that *He Who Loses His Life Will Find It*. See ya 'round." And upon so saying, he started to walk out of the room but he turned for a moment for one final farewell, and for the first time I saw his face...

He was..........Me!

And so, I come to the final pages of this book, but not the ending, for this is where it all began, and there will never be an ending. One who spends his or her life with the young continues to live, even after he or she has left the planet. That is why I have spent my life saying with great pride and gratitude...

I AM A TEACHER

I was born the first moment that a question leaped from the mouth of a child.

I have been many people in many places...

I am Socrates exciting the youth of Athens to discover new ideas through the use of questions.

I am Anne Sullivan tapping out the secrets of the universe into the outstretched hand of Helen Keller.

I am Aesop and Hans Christian Anderson revealing truth through countless stories.

I am Marva Collins fighting for every child's right to an education.

I am Mary McCloud Bethune building a great college for my people, using orange crates for desks.

And I am Bel Kaufman struggling to go *Up the Down Staircase.*

The names of those who have practiced my profession ring like a hall of fame for humanity: Booker T. Washington, Ralph Waldo Emerson, Leo Buscaglia, Buddha, Confucius, Moses, Mohammed and Jesus.

I am also those whose names and faces have long been forgotten, but whose lessons and character will always be remembered in the accomplishments of their students.

I have wept for joy at the weddings of former students, laughed with glee at the birth of their children and stood with head bowed in grief and confusion by graves dug too soon for bodies far too young.

Throughout the course of a day I have been called upon to be an actor, friend, nurse, doctor, coach, finder of lost articles, money lender, taxi driver, psychologist, substitute parent, salesman, politician and keeper of the faith.

Despite the maps, charts, formulas, verbs, stories and books, I have had nothing to teach, for my students really have only themselves to learn, and I know it takes the whole world to tell you who you are.

I am a paradox. I speak loudest when I listen the most. My greatest gifts are in what I am willing to receive from my students.

Material wealth is not one of my goals, but I am a full-time treasure seeker in my quest for new opportunities for my students to use their talents and in my constant search for those talents that sometimes lie buried in self-defeat.

I am the most fortunate of all who labor...

A doctor is allowed to usher life into the world in one magic moment. I am allowed to see that life is reborn each day with new questions, ideas and friendships.

An architect knows that, if he builds with care, his structure may stand for centuries. A teacher knows that if he builds with love and truth, what he builds will last forever.

I am a warrior, daily doing battle against peer pressure, negativity, fear, conformity, prejudice, ignorance and apathy. But I have the greatest allies—Intelligence, Curiosity, Parental Support, Individuality, Creativity, Faith, Love and Laughter—all rushing to my banner with indomitable support.

And whom do I have to thank for this wonderful life I am so fortunate to experience but you, the public, the parents. For you have done me the great honor to entrust to me your greatest contribution to eternity, your children.

And so I have a past that is rich in memories. I have a present that is challenging, adventurous and fun because I am allowed to spend my days with the future.

I am a teacher... and I thank God for it every day.

To enjoy the free online movie portrayal of this, go to:
www.IAmATeacherMovie.com

...to all of the remaining Unsung Heroes – too many to honor and appreciate with just one book.

APPRECIATION

This volume is dedicated to all those magnificent souls whose hearts are bigger than bigotry, whose pride in people put prejudice in its place.

Those who drown hate with hope.

Those seeking school spirit that soars above the clouds of confusion with courage.

Who strive to create a community of humanity that appreciates abilities, builds bridges, creates confidence, delivers dedication and elevates education.

Who heal rather than hurt.

Who delight rather than destroy.

To You, who stand facing the challenge of disease, disaster, loneliness or loss, I wish to say you are not alone.

We bring you companionship. The companionship of others who have walked through tunnels of pain, despair and fear.

When you are filled with doubt and your self-confidence seems a distant memory, look to their light and you will see...

> The Bravery of the Bold,
> The Courage of those who meet Challenge,
> And the Determination of those who faced Death.

When confusion and chaos appear to reign supreme in your life, listen to their wisdom and you will hear the Faith of the Family and Friends. Encouragement fueled by Empathy and the Humor of the Heroic.

We are here to give new life to your soul with fresh insights into love and compassion, which will guide you out of the caverns of solitude. Stories of devotion, fortitude and wisdom will strengthen your resolve.

Our recipe contains a strong dose of inspiration offered by those pursued while walking a path of pain,

Prayed persistently, and...

Those who ascended the summit of survival,

We offer you lighthouses of hope to guide your navigation through the stormy seas.

Tales of those whose loses created a longing, which led to light.

Weariness was used to discover new wisdom.

Confusion caused them to build cathedrals in their souls.

You will gain new energy in your steps and vitality as you embark on this new journey.

And finally, you will be a Miracle Worker—Resurrecting long buried dreams of a nation that gloried in the belief that there are extraordinary possibilities in ordinary people.

Of course we will experience opposition, struggle and adversity from the cynics... people who live lives of desperation, who know the price of everything but the value of nothing.

They have always been there. You've heard their messages spoken throughout history. They said...

To Columbus: "If you sail that far, you'll fall off the earth."

To the Wright Brothers: "Anything heavier than air will crash."

To Winston Churchill: "All of Europe is defeated; you are surrounded and have no natural resources. Give up."

To Rosa Parks: "If you don't sit where we tell you, we'll make sure no one will ever hear of you again."

To Walt Disney: "No adult will sit still for an hour and twenty minutes to watch a cartoon."

To Roger Bannister: "If you run a mile in less than four minutes, your nervous system will collapse under the strain."

To Henry Ford: "You can't make an affordable vehicle that will move without horses."

We stand with them and loudly proclaim...

YOU ARE APPRECIATED!

ABOUT JOHN WAYNE SCHLATTER

John Wayne "Jack" Schlatter is a well loved, deeply respected, and highly acclaimed teacher, author and inspirational speaker. For over 50 years, he has dedicated himself to inspiring, motivating and encouraging young people. During this time he has produced and directed over 200 complete theatrical productions, coached many championship speech teams, and delivered speeches to hundreds of schools and organizations throughout the United States. He can be heard on the tape programs of *Chicken Soup For The Soul*, Vols. 2 and 5, and seen on Career Track's *Chicken Soup For The Soul* Series Video Program

In 1990 he was listed among *Who's Who Among Teachers in America*. Among his credits are school and District *Teacher of the Year* awards, *Kiwanis Teacher of the Year* award, the *Orange County Superintendents Award For Outstanding Contribution To Education*, three *Life-Time PTA* awards, and *Speaker of the Year* in 1993 by the Professional Speakers Network.

He is a man who is as unique as his name implies (he was named after two grandfathers, John Schlatter and Wayne Hoover), whose greatest school was the family in which he was raised. His mother, a classical violinist, toured the United States with William Jennings Bryan, and his father, an outstanding salesman, worked with Vash Young on some of the first positive thinking and self-help books. His brother Bob was a great football coach who turned out many major college and professional players. Brother George is one of the most exceptional TV producers of such classic shows as *Laugh In* and *Real People*, and his "youngest older brother," Alan, was a championship wrestler and an outstanding stock broker.

Jack is available for speeches and workshops with such topics as:

- If You Can Laugh At It, You Can Overcome It
- Let Movie Magic Motivate Your Life
- To Be Great, One Must Learn To Appreciate
- Gifts by the Side of the Road
- Seven Steps to Successful Schools
- Bearers of the Gifts (a tribute to Salesmen)
- The Magic Pebbles
- A New Bill of Rights
- I Am A Teacher - based on his story, which may be the most

widely published work on education over the last 10 years, appearing in *Chicken Soup For The Soul*, Vol.1 and countless reproductions, authorized and otherwise.

To see Jack speak and/or to
schedule a private workshop, keynote or
special presentation with Jack, go to:

~

www.GiftsByTheSideOfTheRoad.com

~

Heart Productions & Publishing
800-639-8191 or 603-382-8848

For general information about Jack's movies,
videos, posters and books, go to:

~

www.MakeADifference.com/Jack

To enjoy ALL of the Free Online Movies and eGreeting Cards
created from the many tributes, acknowledgments and stories
found throughout this book, check these web pages:

~

www.MakeADifference.com/JacksMovies

www.MakeADifference.com/JacksGreetingCards

OR SIMPLY
Get our Free Newsletter and be the
very first to watch them as
they become available. Subscribe at:

~

www.MakeADifference.com/Newsletter

TAKE THE NEXT STEPS WITH HEART PUBLISHING & PRODUCTION

The Simple Gesture, and *I Am A Teacher* Online Movies are part of a series of inspirational movies created by Mary Robinson Reynolds, Founder of Heart Productions & Publishing, with friend and colleague John Wayne "Jack" Schlatter.

For more inspiration from our movies and eGreeting Cards, please visit us at:

www.MakeADifference.com

At our website, you can join our free Make A Difference Newsletter, and watch our inspirational movies daily, to enjoy the benefits of a peaceful, renewed mind, body and spirit.

Popular gift items are available, such as meaningful Jewelry, full color Prints and Motivational Posters, Screensavers, Downloadable Movies and DVDs, "I Make A Difference" Wristbands and Stickers, Online Courses, UTrain™ Programs, Interactive and Inspirational books.

Our Gift to You...

Obtain a Free Download of two Companion Movies for this book,
The Simple Gesture and *I Am A Teacher*, at:

~
www.MakeADifference.com/JacksGifts

Sit back, relax and let Heart Productions & Publishing movies lift you up!
Watch our free flash movies online and
forward them to those you appreciate and care about,
so you can make a difference in someone's life today!

For Quantity Pricing on Book & Posters:

~
www.MakeADifference.com/JacksPricing

info@MakeADifference.com
1-800-639-8191

Make A Difference with the *Gifts by the Side of the Road*
...and we will see World Peace in Our Lifetime